The Little Book of Light Codes

The Little Book of Light Codes

—Healing Symbols of Light—

by

Laara

WAIVER: The author of this book does not dispense medical advice or
other professional advice or prescribe the use of any technique as a form of
diagnosis or treatment for any physical, emotional, or medical condition.
The intent of the author is only to offer information of an anecdotal and
general nature that may be part of your quest for emotional and spiritual
wellbeing. In the event you or others use any of the information or other
content in this book, the author and the publisher assume no responsibility
for the direct or indirect consequences. The reader should consult his
or her medical, health, or other professional before adopting any of the
suggestions in this book or drawing inferences from it.

This book is dedicated to all the brave souls embracing their healing paths.

May your journey be filled with peace and playfulness.

Praise for *The Little Book of Light Codes*

Page after page, my heart was touched in unique, yet familiar, ways. I realized that certain symbols "spoke" to my heart and my "BEing" more strongly than others. I look forward to spending more time with these treasures. What a beautiful gift to share with the world.

—Barbara Hudak, RN BSN MS, Glendale AZ, HeartMath® Certified Senior Trainer and Coach/Mentor

The Little Book of Light Codes offers many beautiful things to start a spiritual journey with: channeled symbols with heart-warming messages, profound meditations, and a basic introduction to working with crystals and sacred objects. It's a self-healing manual for spiritual seekers.

—Sebastian Colbert, Germany

People are hungry for the sacred teachings that Laara has been brave enough to share with us. The symbols within this book harken back to an ancient time. The symbols, their names, and their meanings will fill you with wonder; you will be connected to the timeless sacred again and again.

—Brian Brown, MS, Healer & Computer Programmer, Amherst, WI.

Light Codes offers you simple wisdom as you move forward to a balanced life. They can bring you happiness and fun.

—Rev. Rosalyn L. Bruyere, Founder and Teacher of the
Healing Light Center Church, Medicine Woman,
Master Healer, Arcadia, California

I absolutely love it. I can't really explain it, but some of the symbols made me sway side to side, some made me sit up tall, some made me lean back and open up my heart...I know a lot of people are going to love this book as well!

—Anisette Vestberg, Co-founder of Upgrade
Your Lifestyle Europe, Hoer, Sweden

What appears at first glance to be a charming self-help book offers so much more. If used as instructed, this book has true substance and immense value. It is important to read every page from the beginning of the book onward, adhering to the author's instructions ... then, let the magic amaze you!

—Alison Herod

Nothing glows brighter than the heart awakened to the unseen light of love that lives within it.
—Guy Finley

ACKNOWLEDGMENTS

To my amazing parents, Chuck and Alison Herod, thank you. You have always been a great support to me in all of my endeavors.

To my wonderful teachers, Rosalyn L. Bruyere, Ken Weintrub, and Dr. Stewart Blaikie: Thank you for your guidance, wisdom, patience, and love. My life is forever changed. You have helped bring me back to myself.

To Lady Isis and Jeshua, Light Beings who support us all with incomprehensible Love, thank you for the assistance and energies you put forth in this offering.

To Jesse Krieger and the publishing team at Lifestyle Entrepreneurs Press, thank you for the time, skill, talent, and all the love you put into this book...you have gone above and beyond.

To all my readers, my humble gratitude.

—*Laara*

TABLE OF CONTENTS

Table of contents

Table of contents

PREFACE

How *The Little Book of Light Codes* came to be:

Someone once told me many years ago that Spirit can wake us in the early morning hours to tell us something important, perhaps a message we are missing in our lives. When this began happening to me at 4:00 a.m. during the spring of 2015, I didn't yet see the value of my sleep being disrupted. But that same year, one summer morning, I had an entirely new experience.

When I opened my eyes that morning, I could clearly see five symbols suspended in my inner vision. They were simple, yet intriguing, and I knew I should write them down while I could see them with such detail. I drew them, and went back to sleep. When I looked at the symbols in my journal later that same morning, I felt as though they were trying to tell me something. I felt comforted by them. I was still in the process of navigating my long road of healing a severe back injury after an unfortunate fall from my horse during a show jumping competition in early 2009. Although I was finally getting stronger and my pain was lessening, I still felt depressed, confused, and even frightened as to what my future might bring. I began to feel an interest and a curious pull towards exploring spirituality and various healing modalities. This was a world I had been naturally connected to as a child, but had actively suppressed for years.

As I became more open to receiving, new symbols would present themselves. They would usually appear while I was talking with someone who was sharing their own life struggles. A symbol would appear in my inner vision and I would say, "I'm seeing a symbol that might help you, would you like me to write it down?" I always received a positive (yet curious) response. I would find a scrap piece of paper and a pen and draw what came to me, take a picture of it with my phone, and give the paper to the person, explaining that the symbol would be going in my book. The person would always ask, "Are you going to publish the book?" I would casually respond that it was "a possibility." In *my* reality, however, the book I was creating was simply for myself, I had no real intention of publishing. As I gathered more symbols, I would show them to friends, family, and fellow energy workshop participants, and I started to get the same response from everyone: *You must publish!*

Publishing a book seemed like a pipe dream. I certainly wasn't a writer, nor did I have any idea how to publish anything other than Instagram posts. So here I am, venturing down a whole new, scary, but exciting road. I hope you enjoy these symbols and the accompanying channeled messages. May they comfort you, support you, and assist you in profoundly healing ways. May they show you the guidance and connection you long for, and remind you of the infinite love, wisdom, and light you hold within yourself.

Love, Laara
Victoria, B.C. Canada

FOREWORD

As we each continue our own unique adventure, individual and global collective consciousness expands and new paradigms evolve in the quantum fields of awareness. For those evolving souls who are optimizing their conscious experience in the third dimension here and now, *The Little Book of Light Codes* offers incredible opportunities to create coherence with Heart and Mind. Each highly-charged Light Code symbol in this book offers you huge transformational possibilities on the energetic, emotional, mind, and soul levels—on both the inner and outer planes.

I highly recommend this book to anyone on a healing journey. Are you wrestling with difficult life issues personally? Are you ready to expand and upgrade your Love and Light to optimize your health and happiness? If your answers to these questions is "Yes!" ... *then this book is for you.* As you work with the fifty-two coded, channeled symbols and Laara's guided meditations, they will resonate with your infinite and magical potential to transform your life. You will discover the open, expansive, sacred healing space within and around these symbols, which goes beyond the logical and mundane into the world of fascinating wonders and new possibilities.

For practitioners drawn to help others on their healing path, this book offers a valuable framework for creating transformational healing sessions with each of the fifty-two channeled symbols.

I am honored to invite all readers to explore their deeper truths, to awaken to a new healing paradigm, and to harness the healing power of the universe with *The Little Book of Light Codes*. May this book enrich, empower, and bless your journey.

Dr. Stewart Blaikie
Victoria, B.C.

INTRODUCTION

Welcome to *The Little Book of Light Codes*

The symbols in this book are channeled, living energies of healing Codes of Light from the Universe, designed to help human beings along on our unique and individual paths. Each symbol has its own character and personality and each offers us unique gifts, including DNA repair, upgrades, and activations. Each symbol is associated with a channeled message that I have written down (these have been edited from the original for clarity and readability), and have been assembled in a progressive manner that makes the symbols and their meanings understood more easily.

Most of the symbols in this book have a unique name to describe their particular healing frequency. In some cases, however, only an English word or phrase is used to describe certain symbols. This is because no universal name was accorded to the symbol during the channeling process.

I recommend that you move through the symbols in this book in the order they are presented. In the event that you find yourself curious as to what might come next, please refrain from moving forward in the book out of order. Also, if you feel stuck with a symbol and the seven-day period has not yet passed, that's a sign that you should stay with it. After seven days, you may move on. You may find yourself drawn to a particular symbol one day, and feel resistance towards it the next, depending upon what energies, stressors, or triggers you are working with in your life. You may even find yourself rejecting the symbol that you need to engage with the most!

As you work with the messages, wisdom, and frequencies expressed by each symbol, your process with *The Little Book of Light Codes* will be as personalized and as healing as you choose. Although the descriptions related to each sigil are sometimes short, the energy frequency each symbol emits and the information each offers is infinite. Know that simply by looking at a symbol, you will gain information your soul is seeking in order to perfect itself and reflect Divine Love. As you move through this book, you may experience release, change, and even total transformation in your physical, mental, emotional, or spiritual bodies. *Just flow with it!*

I recommend that to maximize your experience, you work with these symbols from a calm and centered space. But they will work with anyone at any time as long as the user is willing to engage fully and authentically with them. In most sections, I have included an exercise to help you attune with each symbol. But the suggestions I offer are simply to get you started. There is plenty of room for self-exploration. As you progress, there will be opportunities to expand on how you relate to and work with the symbols—and the symbols themselves may show you unique approaches to harness their power. Follow your inner guidance and intuition, and trust the unfolding. Remember, each person has the freedom to discover for themselves how to work with each symbol for their highest good. Enjoy!

General Information:

As noted, the symbols are Universal Codes of Light which anyone can work with at any time. The transformational potential of the symbols is limitless...the only limits are the limits you place upon yourself. The Universal Intelligence within each symbol's forms and curves is condensed and compacted, allowing your soul to integrate a mass of information simply by beholding each shape's contours and lines. You may use the healing energy of the symbols for yourself or for others, but remember—the information and healing properties of the symbols cannot be forced upon anyone against their will or in contravention of their highest good.

As human beings, we have forgotten who we are and what our purpose is—we are caught in an illusory web of separation and lack, filled with confusion, pain, and suffering. The symbols hold healing frequencies and messages of Love which every person knows innately but is seeking to remember. We can trust that the symbols' counsel will guide us back to a place of self-realization, where we can reawaken our limitless capacity for Love. We can reclaim our Heart-centered connection to one another and begin once again to tap into the truth of who we are: spiritual beings having a human experience.

The symbols do not violate the tenets of any spiritual belief system or religious doctrine. They are expressions of Love. They help the user to release and work through fears, limiting beliefs, traumas, vulnerabilities, and lack of confidence, with the intention of healing and bringing forth the Love we hold within. When we engage with these symbols, they will only work as deeply as we wish them to work, they will only assist us in releasing what is safe and appropriate, and they will only operate in alignment with the highest good for the user and in the highest good of all.

Instructions:

For maximum benefit, as noted, I recommend you work with the symbols in the order presented in this book. Their structure is arranged for systematic healing, working towards the resetting of beliefs, perception, confusion, and disease. While there is no maximum recommended amount of time for working with any symbol, it is recommended that you work with each symbol for *not less than seven days* before moving on to the next symbol. Once you have worked with a symbol for seven days or more, you may visit it again whenever necessary, and then resume your place within the book. You may work with the symbols in this book as many times as you like.

Intention-Setting:

We are thinking, feeling, conscious, creative human beings with the capacity to make what we think a reality. In fact, our conscious brains don't know the difference between an imagined event and a "real" event. This means that when we intend to manifest certain things in our lives, it is important to be clear, specific, and detailed in our intentions *and* to engage with our physical senses as we hold an intention in our conscious minds. In order for our intentions to have momentum, we must engage at least two (and preferably more) of our physical senses simultaneously. We must see, hear, feel, smell, and even taste the thing we intend to create. The more senses we can engage, the more real our intention becomes, and the more likely it is to manifest in physical form.

So, we need to *choose* (as our act of intention-setting) to work with these symbols in an honorable way, bringing forth our most excellent selves to the best of our ability. Remember, there is no pressure, just do your best to accept yourself, for who you are and where you are on any given day. Showing up is half the battle. When you work with a symbol, be clear in your intention that you are choosing to heal that which no longer serves you, making room within your being for more Love, happiness, health, and abundance!

Instructions on Grounding:
The majority of the symbols in *The Little Book of Light Codes* offer a meditation as part of their healing process. You are asked to relax and sink deeply into the earth while slowing your breath. When we ground before we begin our healing practice through meditation, it enhances our ability to open up to new information, release old energies, and anchor elevated feelings into our bodies so we may

begin to lead a more joyful and fulfilling life. This book recommends the specific grounding technique below. You can use it each time you begin your practice with the symbols. It engages the minor chakras on the bottoms of the feet, and will help you to center and ground so you will be better able to attune with the vibrational frequency of the symbols.

Grounding Practice:
Sit in a chair with your feet flat on the floor. Relax. Breathe slowly. On each inhale, imagine that your feet are suction cups, pulling energy up from the earth. On each exhale, relax. With each inhale, imagine your feet pulling energy up from the earth, through the floor, into your legs. Feel the energy moving up within your body with each in-breath, until it reaches the top of your head. Release it out of the top of your head (or *crown chakra*). Imagine the energy flowing out like a waterfall. Practice this grounding exercise often, so it becomes second nature. Use this process at the beginning of your meditation practice; it will help center you and prepare you to enter any level of awareness you may wish to access. Grounding connects your Heart and mind. It can promote wellness, improve sleep, lower your blood pressure, and reduce stress and anxiety—it's a great way to start and end each day!

Meditations:
You can interact with the symbols in *The Little Book of Light Codes* by using the meditations described below the

symbols. These meditations may be done with your eyes open or closed as you feel comfortable, but sitting down is suggested, to facilitate relaxation. It is recommended that you begin with your grounding practice before starting this meditation, and it can be helpful to finish your meditation with the same grounding practice to bring you back into your body, ready for the rest of your day. (Note: not every symbol has a corresponding meditation. For these symbols, simply contemplate the related text, and, when you feel connected to the meaning of the symbol, if you wish, incorporate your favorite meditation into your session. How you work with each symbol will be personal to you.)

Before beginning any meditation, hold your arms out at shoulder height. This is the approximate size of your aura, and the edge of the energy field you will be feeling into during the meditation. Embrace the sensation of blending the energy of the symbol with your auric field and allow the healing Light of the symbol to penetrate your being and raise your vibration!

Six Direction Meditation Instructions:
Once you feel the energy of the earth flowing up from the bottoms of your feet into your body and out the top of your head, take your awareness to your back. Feel into the space behind you, about an arm's length in distance, while continuing to pull energy from the earth into your feet and out the top of your head. Maintain a connection with your back, and bring your attention to the sides of your body. Feel about an arm's length in distance into the space around your side-body. Continue pulling energy into your feet and out the top of your head. Then, bring

your attention to your front-body while maintaining the connection to your back and sides, feeling approximately an arm's length into the space in front of you. Next, bring your attention to your feet, allowing yourself to feel into the ground again, to a depth of about an arm's length. While pulling energy into your feet and out the top of your head, bring your attention to the space above your head, about three feet above you. Now, feel the space behind you, beside you, in front of you, deep into the earth, and above your head simultaneously. Continue to bring energy up from the earth into your feet and out the top of your head. When you are ready, bring your attention back to your feet, and to the energy flowing through your body. Gently open your eyes.

This is a wonderful meditation to prepare you for working with any of the symbols in this book. Simply do this meditation, then open your eyes and look at the symbol. You will be open and able to receive the healings, messages, upgrades, and frequencies necessary for you.

Clarification of Terms:
Our Many Minds—In spirituality, the word "mind" can be used to describe several minds: The Ego mind, the Heart mind, the Soul mind, and the Universal mind.

Ego Mind
The ego, or the lower-self, is the physical, incarnated self you as a soul have come to learn through. It is the

name you answer to, and it is responsible for expressing reactions and "lower" feelings such as guilt, shame, blame, jealousy, fear, hatred, etc. Our ego is an essential part of being human, as it is your expression of individuality. The ego is not bad. We need it in order to be who we are as a soul living a human life on this planet. However, for many people, the ego has become out of balance with the Heart, suppressing the Heart so we forget what is most important: Love.

Heart Mind

When the heart is mentioned throughout this book, we are referring to our energetic Heart, rather than our physical heart. Our Hearts have an intelligence, a mind. Our Hearts are our connection to our Soul mind and to "All That Is." When our Heart and ego are in balance, the ego supports the Heart rather than suppresses it. The ego answers our Heart's desires, by bringing forth in excellence the intelligence of our brain, allowing us to work in harmony with the Heart's wisdom and its ultimate connection to All That Is. Our Hearts are in alignment with the Light.

Soul Mind

The soul is a collection of Light frequencies: Love vibrations which hold within them our individual, ultimate, supreme consciousness. The soul is wise, connected, and knowing. It seeks to grow and expand to know itself in a deeper, grander sense, and it does so by manifesting various expressions of itself as living entities. The "mind of the soul" refers to the vast expression and knowledge which are gathered, in part, by the soul's experiences throughout each lifetime. If we are able to heal at a soul level and connect with ourselves and others authentically, we are communicating in ultimate Truth, in Love. To attain self-mastery is to know oneself—and to know oneself is to know the soul.

Universal Mind

The universal mind is also referred to with names like Source, God, Creator, or with other similar terms. This is the energy of All That Is, it is the fabric of the interconnected web of consciousness. The universal mind is all-inclusive. It is the soul mind of humanity as well as the collective mind of all beings. We all have access to the universal mind, as we are all made of this mind. The universal mind is the very stuff of life, it is the network that links us to one another, to nature, to the earth, to the cosmos, and beyond. We *are* each a part of and the whole of the universal mind.

Light and Love
"Light" vs. "light"

When light is described within the context of this book, we are referring to Divine Light. Divine Light is the Light of "All That Is;" source energy, or universal energy. It is God's Light, it is *your* infinite Light. Your Light is the *Love that you are.*

"Love" vs. "love"

Love as an action (loving or to love) is different than the Love that you are, your true, authentic self. We capitalize Love throughout this book when we are referring to the *truth* of who you are, your essence or Soul Light, and Universal/Source/God-Love.

Cleansing a Crystal or Sacred Object:

There may be occasions when it is helpful for us to work with crystals or other sacred objects. When we acquire such an object, it is important to cleanse the object of any negative energies, so we can receive the loving support we require without hindrance. There are several ways to clear lower energies from an object, and it is important to choose what is most appropriate for you and the material you are cleansing. Remember to be clear with your intentions, requesting that all negative energy be released from the object and be transmuted for the highest good of all.

Salt

Salt is the most accessible compound for cleansing an object. Both ocean water and table salt are very effective at clearing lower vibrational energies. Salt should not be used for all materials, however. Some crystals will dissolve in salt water, so it is important to do research on the material you wish to cleanse. If you feel you need to use salt with an object that cannot be submerged in salt water, simply place the object on top of a small pile of dry salt on your countertop.

Moonlight
Some people enjoy taking their crystals or other sacred objects out under the light of a full moon for cleansing. Simply take your object into the moonlight; you'll be harnessing the purging and clearing energies the full moon provides. Request that the energies be released from the object and that the moonlight transmute them into positive energies for the highest good of all.

Sunlight
Sunlight is another powerful means of clearing, but again, it isn't for every object. Some crystals will fade in color if exposed to too much direct sunlight. Place your object in the light of the sun, and state your good intentions for its clearing.

Fire
We can use the flame of a candle to cleanse objects. Carefully hold the object above the flame, at enough distance so you don't burn yourself or your object. Request that the object be cleared of all negative energies and transmuted by the light of the flame.

I am honored to bring these many symbols to humanity at this time of great change and healing. I feel an immense amount of gratitude and appreciation for the Light Beings who have collaborated with my soul on this mission, including the powerful and magical energies of Lady Isis and Jeshua.

The Little Book of Light Codes' beautiful accompanying Oracle Cards and Journal are intended to assist you further on your healing journey. You may find journaling your process with *The Little Book of Light Codes* very helpful—and fun to look at later, so you may see the transformations you've made. The Oracle Cards are intended to share with you some of the beautiful color frequencies emitted by each symbol, and to serve as a supplement to the course-like process intended with this book. It is recommended that you use the Oracle Cards by matching each card with the related symbol in the book, to help you to integrate the healings presented to you.

I hope you enjoy *The Little Book of Light Codes*, the Oracle Cards, and the Journal. Have fun!

All blessings,
—*Laara*

Reader Reminder

Please read and work with the symbols in the order in which they are presented. Allow a minimum of one week to work with each symbol, giving yourself the space to relax, contemplate, and integrate the sacred teachings offered. Enjoy!

—Laara

Lakahana

(Lah-kah-ha-nah)

Embody Love and Harmony, Trust Yourself and Others, Release Fear

We all have the ability to find and embody the Love that we are. Everyone is Love; everyone is an expression of Love. Yet when we are faced with actions that suggest otherwise, or when we are witness to suffering or aggression, this can be confusing. We can get caught in the illusions of the world that draw us away from our natural state of Love. In our absence from Love, we can experience illness, sorrow, fear, anxiety—and endure many other illusory circumstances that seem contrary to Love. However, we have the power to choose to work through our dis-eases, programs, beliefs, fears, and disharmonies and to remember ourselves as Beings of Love. It is our choice to heal. It is our choice to open our Hearts, do our work, and strive to love ourselves and others unconditionally.

Our Hearts have an infinite capacity to love. Our Hearts connect to everyone and everything. Our Hearts hold great wisdom and strength and when they have the opportunity to give from a genuine, aligned place, they give freely and abundantly. When we do our inner work, we are working towards living life from our Hearts. Like peeling back the layers of an onion, eventually we find our center—our Heart—unencumbered now by the layers of confusion which once distorted it, preventing it from working in the magic of the Light. There is no more fear, no more struggle. There is only Love and peace.

Lakahana expresses that you are capable of peeling back layers of false beliefs, disharmony, and dis-ease. This is a process of self-discovery; you can heal with a sense of lightness. Although you may face challenging times along the way, the journey is exactly that—a journey of love, towards Love. This symbol represents your Heart, conveying its desire to be free from pain and suffering. For beneath the layers of pain and the illusions of separation and acts of violence which mask it, your Heart is happy.

This sigil is an offering of trust: trust that you can release fear, trust that you can heal, and trust that you are actively healing. Stay true to what feels good and right for you. Don't be swayed by falsities or external circumstances. Your Heart has all the answers you could ever need. It is time to listen more closely. The voice you hear is soft...it is yours.

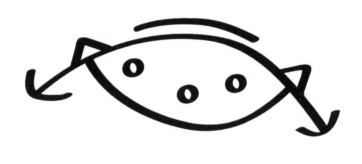

Gamma

(Gam-mah)

Opening Channels of Light, Connecting to Source, Breaking Through, Dissolving Barriers

Happiness, sweetness, lightness, and playfulness: Gamma comes to you with a message of joy! Whatever your current situation or struggle might be, Gamma reminds you that there is another perspective to view it from, another choice you can make, or another solution that will soon present itself. When we shed light on something, it always looks different than it did in the dark. There is a positive intent in every situation... sometimes the challenge is in finding it!

Even if you feel you are a victim of negative circumstances, there is potential for positive gain. It is your choice. Always. Gamma reminds us that we can look at something in a different way, with more awareness, ease, and even happiness! It reminds us that there is Love to be found even in the darkest places. We need only remember to bring forward our Light.

Look gently upon Gamma. Look for and feel into its unique playfulness, sweetness, and compassion. There is a spark of Light in every dark space—choose to see it! Perhaps you notice something beautiful near you, or something that makes you laugh. As you travel the path of Self-Love, Gamma reminds you not to try so hard, and not to be hard on yourself. Gamma offers you strength and stamina, so you can clear away any barrier or challenge that has impeded your movement ever closer towards embracing joy.

Sit quietly and comfortably in a place you won't be disturbed. Close your eyes and quiet your mind. With every slow, deep breath you take, feel yourself sinking deeply into the ground. When you are ready, open your eyes and gaze softly upon Gamma. Feel its happiness and sweetness. Feel it gently guiding you into a lighter, more joyful place. Feel yourself open to its guidance and assistance on your healing journey. Stay with Gamma for as long as is comfortable. When you are done, thank Gamma for its assistance. Use this symbol as often as you feel is right for you.

Yah'kma

(Yah-k-mah, with a break before the 'k')

Creating a Sacred Healing Space

In order for healing to occur, we must feel safe. We must create a space conducive to healing, a place our nervous systems recognize as secure, soothing, and nurturing. Suffering occurs with discomfort, so we must find comfort!

A sacred healing space can take many forms. Ultimately, healing must happen within us, but before this can occur naturally, we need to create healing surroundings. If it's possible, dedicate a place (or even an entire room) in your home for healing.

When working with this symbol, it does not matter what the root of our pain or suffering might be—for Yah'kma, all pain is equal, whether it be emotional, physical, mental, or spiritual, or a combination of these. As long as we choose to work with this sigil for our highest good, Yah'kma brings in an energy to support us on our journey towards wellbeing, away from pain and suffering. When we work with Yah'kma, we move from a state of suffering into a nurturing, supportive, Light-filled existence.

As you work with this symbol, hold the intention of generating health and wellness. See yourself living an optimistic, healthy, and happy life, free of pain and suffering. This symbol works well to facilitate your healing process when you chant its name: *Yah'kma*. Try to hesitate a bit before pronouncing the "k," but do not worry about pronouncing it perfectly. Chant *Yah'kma* in your healing space. Alternatively, meditate while gazing at the symbol, softly and gently saying its name. Drawing Yah'kma on a special piece of paper and placing it on an altar or nightstand is also a way to bring its energy into your space.

Akahanama

(Ah-kah-ha-nah-mah)

Freedom to Choose, Freedom to Release, Freedom to Be the Love that You Are

Akahanama displays the energetic expression of what it is to be free within your own being. Like your true essence, Akahanama is carefree, flowing, light, expressive, and loving. When we make conscious choices from a place of Love, we are acting rightly and respectfully, in harmony with ourselves and those around us, and in support of our highest good and the highest good of all. Akahanama encourages us to do what is in full alignment for us, and what is in integrity for all. Doing our inner work to release the illusions of *what we are not* will allow us to work towards embracing our *authentic selves*. By doing our work, we honor ourselves as the Love that we are, and we revere the beings of Love all around us.

Akahanama asks you to be brave, to take a chance on something that deep down you want to do, change, or be, as you work towards discovering your genuine self. The universe loves and supports you fully, so take a chance on yourself! You know better than anyone what will make you truly happy. Relax. Look around you. This is your life, no one else's. It is your birthright to be who you came to this planet to be: an authentic expression of the Love that you are. How lucky we are to have you here! You have much to share and contribute. Keep Akahanama close to you as a reminder to let go of what scares you, what suppresses you, and what inhibits you from being free— free to choose, free to be, free to discover, and free to embrace the Love that you are.

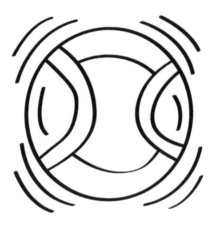

Yah'tkh

(Yaa-tuck)

"Just Be" – Being Centered and Grounded with Integrity and Inner Strength

As we move forward on our healing journey, we notice how life seems to be easier when we have a stillness about us. In order to reach this place of peace, we must be strong within ourselves and find our center, where everything is perfect. There is no worry, stress, or pain here. There is only acceptance. We feel a great sense of integrity as we embrace our grounded and centered nature.

Yah'tkh works in two ways: it can help you focus your energy inward as you center yourself, and it can guide you as you expand your energy outward, to infinity. These are two seemingly opposite actions, but both are necessary to learn as we gain the ability to work with our energetic field. As above, so below. As within, so without. The peace we find inside ourselves is universal peace.

If you feel panicked, anxious, or overwhelmed, you are off center…you need to ground yourself. If you are feeling lost or you are caught up in the events in your own world, unable to see your situation from multiple angles or to recognize the solutions available to you, focus on Yah'tkh. Yah'tkh will help you find a more centered state of being, and will call forth your immense capacity of strength and resilience.

Yah'tkh asks you to take a moment to slow down. Sit quietly and break through your thoughts, settling your mind. Breathe slowly and deeply, allowing yourself to sink into the ground with every exhale. When you feel ready, ask yourself: "Where is my stillpoint?" To help you locate it, rest your gaze upon the Yah'tkh symbol. Simply trust and allow the experience to unfold. Gently feel for the calm, smooth frequencies the symbol emits. When you are ready, turn your attention inward while still gazing at the symbol. Let go of your physical senses, and contemplate the stillness within. Then, allow Yah'tkh to show you the way of infinite expansion. This process will help you remain in a state of grace, even in the most challenging situations. When you are finished exploring, gently bring yourself back into your body by breathing deeply and feeling your feet and legs. Wiggle your fingers and toes. Kindly thank Yah'tkh for its assistance.

Rugth

(Roo-g-th)

Being Centered and Grounded, Gently Maintaining Respectful Boundaries

When circumstances and interactions with others trigger us emotionally, our reactions can sometimes knock us off center. We can feel vulnerable, upset, even hopeless. In these moments, we give our power away. Whenever something causes us dis-ease in this way, it is an invitation to us to look at a deeper issue. What is really going on? Rugth can support us to find the root cause of our dis-ease, re-establish our personal power, and create healthy boundaries. It is especially useful while doing shadow work. It creates momentum, re-sets the energies, and shifts our perspective about how we deserve to experience life: full of Love, respect, and kindness.

Rugth is a power symbol. It can be used to invoke potent boundary energies in your living space, work space, and even within your being. To bring forth these energies, begin by sitting comfortably with the symbol in front of you. Breathe slowly and deeply. With each inhalation, feel a sense of calm washing over you. With every exhalation, feel yourself sinking deeper and deeper into the earth. Set your intention in your own words, describing how you wish to utilize this symbol to bring forth centered, grounded, gently respectful boundaries within and around you. Softly contemplate Rugth while looking upon the symbol and feeling your affirmation intensify. Stay with this energy until you feel the blessings of Rugth revitalizing you. Then, quietly thank Rugth for helping you discover how to tap into the deepest truth of who you are.

Alternatively, or in addition to the meditation offered above, you may wish to draw Rugth on a special piece of paper or on a card, and place it in any area you feel needs to be grounded or centered, or in which you want to create healthy boundaries.

Scryb'th

(Scrib-th)

Warming the Heart, Supporting a Healthy Path, Expanding Self

Over time, our Heart becomes restricted as we guard ourselves against hurts and traumas. The defences we build to protect our Heart add to the challenge of accessing our Heart's wisdom. Without this wisdom, we struggle to discover the choices that are in full alignment with our highest good. The best way to connect with what is in our highest good is through our Heart! If we want to experience abundance and joy in our daily lives, we must find a way to move freely into our Heart space again!

As we feel into our Heart, our inner Light begins to shine a little brighter. We find greater access to our inner knowing while we align with our truth, and we step further into the space that life holds for us as our birthright. We learn not to dim our Light. We discover that it is safe to shine brightly! When our Heart expands, our Light becomes brighter, and we embrace, more and more, the Love that we are.

Scryb'th asks us to remember our Heart. Many of us have used our minds to build walls and barriers around ourselves in an effort to protect our Heart. But Scryb'th reminds us that our Heart is capable…it does not need the false protection our minds try to provide. This symbol

41

suggests that it is time to dismantle the walls we have constructed. We can trust that our Heart can and will be healed. We can choose to remember our power and the miracles within and around us.

Scryb'th supports your healing journey and helps to ignite your potential. As you work with it, it offers you safety and sanctuary. Notice your being-ness expanding. Embrace the freedom and change this symbol provides. You may find that your intuition becomes clearer after engaging with Scryb'th. Listen to your Heart for guidance. Your Heart knows what is best for you in all aspects of your life. As you sit with the symbol, ask from your Heart: "What is in my highest good?" Then, listen for the answer! Sometimes answers appear in the most mysterious places!

Sit quietly and comfortably, with Scryb'th in front of you. Close your eyes. Breathe deeply. With each breath, feel yourself sinking deeper and deeper into the ground. Place one or both hands over your heart-center (heart chakra). Feel your hands against your chest. Feel into your heart space. When you are ready, open your eyes and look at the symbol. Ask for your Heart to heal, gently but swiftly. Imagine your Heart expanding. Feel the lightness filling you up. Feel yourself reconnecting to source. Your Heart is so much more powerful than you imagine! Be patient and kind to yourself, as this healing is profound. Remember, by healing yourself, you are helping to heal everyone and everything. As you gaze upon Scryb'th, hear it speaking to your Heart.

Ahagma

(Ah-ha-g-mah)

Integrating, Taking the Next Step, Releasing Resistance, Making Progress

Interacting with and reminiscing about the past is a choice we make. Dwelling in the past prevents us from living life fully and experiencing the potential blessings and offerings the world holds for us. Living in the past keeps it alive...it keeps us from living in the *now*. Sometimes we don't know how to move forward, and we get stuck in the trenches of discomfort. By honoring our past but not "living there," we can heal.

Healing is a process of discovery, forgiveness, and acceptance. Part of moving forward within the healing process is integrating and releasing past events, traumas, and resistance. This affords us the opportunity to heal completely, and to become engaged in living life from a more fulfilling place.

Ahagma helps us to integrate our lessons, our healings, and our experiences. By assimilating all of our experiences, we can continue forward along our path, empowered, uplifted, and inspired. Ahagma encourages you to be brave, to take that next step. It wants to help you release any resistance you feel...whether it is manifesting as anger, fear, sadness, or any other form of confusion.

This symbol honors you and reminds you that every choice you make is okay, that experience is what life is all about. Feel what you feel and stay with your feelings as long as you need to; there is never a rush. When you are ready to move forward and embrace what you have learned, Ahagma is waiting to assist you with the momentum, Love, and acceptance you require.

Ahagma guides you into the next stage of your process with a lightness and ease. It asks you to trust in the unfolding and timing of the universe, but reminds you that in order to live a happy, peaceful, Heart-centered life, you must participate actively. When you go within and connect with your true self, your life flows with your rhythms, in your time, with your Love.

Sit quietly and comfortably with this sigil before you. Breathe deeply. Relax. While gazing gently upon Ahagma, hold positive, clear intentions for releasing what needs to be released, integrating what needs to be integrated, and moving forward along your journey in excellence. You need not know the details of how this process will unfold or how your healing will occur. Sit for as long as you need to. When you are finished, offer gratitude to Ahagma, to the universe, and to yourself.

If you are using this book as a course, it is recommended that you do not proceed onto the next symbol until you have consciously committed to letting the past remain in the past. Your future is bright and the universe supports you and loves you in all your endeavors.

Kh'mak

(K'mac)

Time, Presence, Flow, Freedom, Breath

Kh'mak is a symbol of freedom, breath, flow, presence, and time. Only the current, present moment matters. This symbol suggests that you make a conscious effort to be in the now. If you feel confined or restricted in some area of your life, no matter how challenging the circumstance might be, the best way to navigate it is by grounding and being present with it. Many of us use distraction to avoid what makes us uncomfortable but when we do this, we place limits on ourselves. For example, if we have trouble breathing, we are immediately present to our dilemma...our minds are focused, not wandering. It is only by being present that we can overcome the obstacle that life is presenting us. Thus, whether we need to breathe freely or simply free ourselves from life's trials and tribulations, we do not give up on difficult situations or abandon our commitments. We still take full responsibility for ourselves. Kh'mak's message is to find space (expansive breath) and to flow through our existence. We find in doing this that the reward for living in the present moment is *freedom*. Through practicing working with the present moment, we can develop skills which allow us to move through challenging experiences. Our gain is (hopefully) a lesson learned!

Kh'mak brings a clear message: Slow down. There is potentially something in your current perception which it would serve you well to notice. As noted, this symbol is about time, freedom, and flow. When you are in flow, you are free...you are not resisting the life that is unfolding before you. Take a deep breath. Notice what is going on around and within you. Nothing matters but the current moment. Be with yourself, however you have shown up today in all of your perfection.

Sit quietly and comfortably with this symbol before you. Relax. Breathe deeply. Close your eyes for a moment. Once you feel calm and peaceful, gaze gently upon Kh'mak. Ask the energies of this symbol to show you areas in your life that need adjusting, and be open to the many ways the information can be presented. Look for opportunities to become a more conscious participant in your life. Kh'mak knows your capabilities and has unlimited faith in your success.

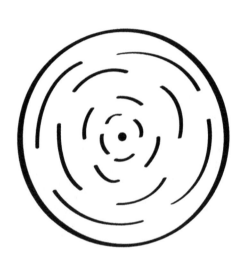

Turla

(Tour-la)

Stillpoint

The emotional reactions we have to challenges in our lives can produce a chaotic energy. The more volatile we are, the more we react, and the more erratic our energy becomes. We get caught in an escalating loop of chaos. This growing dysfunctional and reactive emotional state can pose some difficulty for us in returning to our calm, centered state of being. Thus, how we handle challenging times (whether a single moment or a long series of moments) determines our quality of life. For example, if we react to a situation and it takes a day (or longer) for us to "let it go," we've lost our ability to experience life from a beautiful, enjoyable state of mind. What happens when we see the world through a lens of anger, bitterness, fear, or jealousy? We might ask ourselves if it's worth giving up our happiness and joy so we can be miserable about or towards something, or just so we can feel justified about the wrongness we perceive.

Since we are what we practice, when we are accustomed to being far outside of peace, our ability to find peace can be a challenge. However, within each of us is a beautiful stillpoint. We all have the ability to access this point, a home which is truly ours and is always available to us. When we remember how to locate this stillpoint—our center—the chaos of the external world disappears. We gain the ability to navigate challenging situations with greater ease, compassion, and understanding. When we do get triggered, if we come back to our stillpoint, the charge of the trigger melts away and we have the opportunity to navigate the situation with ease! The more we practice non-reactivity, the less reactive we become, and the more harmony we restore to the energy within our lives.

Sit quietly with Turla before you. Close your eyes and as you slow your breath, find yourself sinking deeper into the ground. Turla wishes to assist you in remembering your stillpoint, the point within you which is calm, relaxed, and an expression of your infinite Love. This is the point of connection to your wisdom, and your connection to all things. Sit with Turla and gently settle your gaze on the symbol, allowing it to take you deep within yourself. Practice this often, so that finding your stillpoint becomes second nature for you. When you find yourself in any challenging situation, try taking a moment before responding. Take a deep breath, find your stillpoint, and be ready and open for the possibilities. With a little practice, you may find yourself surprised at the changes which can occur around you.

Tsuhami

(Tsu-ha-mi)

Butterfly Wings: Spread Your Wings and Fly, Release Resistance, Trust

When we begin to release that which restricts us, we become lighter, more confident, more positive. This is our opportunity to find our wings and gently, gracefully, and with strength and beauty, take flight. Like a butterfly, we can float and fly from flower to flower, in search of that which will feed our soul.

Tsuhami offers you the energetic feeling of opening and stretching your soft wings further than you may have in a long time (or potentially, more than you ever have before). Trust that your wings will keep you aloft as you continue to release bitter emotions or memories and find more places and situations that provide sweet, nourishing nectar.

Tsuhami also comes with a message: *You have done good work within yourself, you have awakened your true power. It is time to take the next step. It is time to let go, free yourself, and live your highest purpose. It is time to transform yourself from what you once were to what you are becoming. You must find the right flowers in the right gardens to nourish and support you so you can grow, flourish, and step into the miraculous life you were meant to live.*

Sit quietly and comfortably with Tsuhami in front of you. Relax. Breathe deeply and slowly, allowing yourself to sink into the ground. Bring your soft gaze to the symbol. Quietly sense the energy radiating from the back of your body, three feet out into the space behind you, out into space. Then, pay attention to your feet...feel yourself sinking ever more deeply into the earth. Now, notice the back of your body again. Feel for your wings. They are there. Once you have connected with them, sit with them for a moment.

Continue now to look at the symbol. Tsuhami offers you many blessings at this time...it offers more nectar in your life. Feel your Heart soften as you open to its sweetness. Receive as much pure, loving energy as you can into your Heart, knowing that you will receive the perfect amount for you. When you are finished, feel your wings spreading. Say, "I choose a life full of nourishment and sweetness now. Thank you, Tsuhami for your blessings."

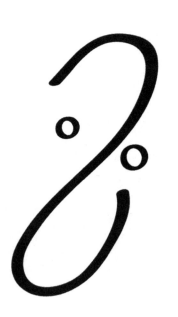

Turmar

(Toor-mar)

Unity

Turmar vibrates with the frequency of unity in Self, helping you to establish a stronger connection and communication with your higher self. To connect with this energy, we must dismantle our egos. When we seek to align with the unifying forces of Oneness, there is an acceptance and flow, and a movement towards the expansion of our Heart. This can be confusing because so often we are told we will find Oneness through stillness...which is also true. However, to arrive at a place of stillness, we must also learn to flow, for "still" is not "stagnant." Turmar helps us to find our flow within, to tap into our spiritual selves, and to move beyond the limitations of the physical world. It helps us to surrender the ego, to locate our Heart-based living, and to discover the sense of unity we seek. When we engage with Turmar, we cease to seek outside of ourselves for answers, and instead, we access our inner knowing and embrace Self-Love. Loneliness ends, we feel connected to everyone and All That Is. We begin to have a sense of purpose, life takes on new meaning, and we feel called to action.

Turmar offers a simple meditation to help us find the flow and process of releasing the ego, allowing us to connect further with our higher selves. It is from this place that we will find ourselves more easily accessing a connection to All, with our Heart leading the way in gratitude and compassion.

Sit with the Turmar symbol near you. Close your eyes. As you slow and deepen your breath, feel yourself sinking into the ground. Quiet your mind. When you are ready, open your eyes and gaze at Turmar. Ask Turmar to show you the path towards a life of unity with all beings of Light. You may also ask Turmar for help in releasing the false control of your ego, and direction on how to increase your connection and communication with your higher self. Close your eyes again. Keep your requests and intentions clear in your mind for a while, then softly let them go. Gaze upon Turmar again, this time opening yourself up to the energies and guidance this symbol gifts you with today. Stay with this energy, then thank Turmar for its loving counsel.

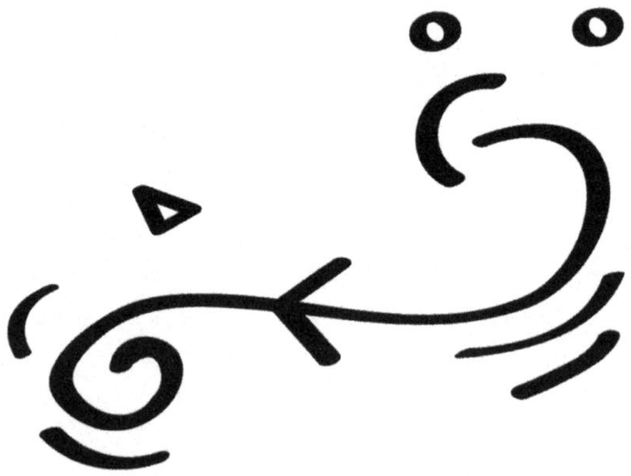

Teglih

(Teg-li)

Healing the Physical Plane (Mother Earth, Her Plants, and the Physical Body)

As compassionate souls, we human beings feel compelled to offer blessings of healing when we see suffering around us. Whether our prayers are for other human beings, plants, animals, countries, or the entire planet, we look for ways to be a positive support.

Teglih is a symbol of healing and is not limited by time or space. Governed by the laws of quantum physics, the energy of Teglih can be used non-locally, which means that the physical location of the healer or subject is not a limiting factor. Its healing vibration can be used on anyone or anything, at any time, simply by bringing the recipient into your conscious mind. The energetic healing power of Teglih can be applied in several ways: in person, by looking at a photograph of the individual you are sending healing intentions to, or from a distance, simply by sensing the person and intuitively drawing their energetic presence into your own energy field.

Teglih is also a symbol of blessing. Speaking the name "Teglih" aloud is powerful, and it can be incorporated into prayer. This symbol's gentle offering of healing can be included in works of art, or can be featured in a frame in an office space where passersby might notice it. Its frequency is high, but still accessible for most people. If its vibration is too strong for someone, they will simply not resonate with it and will look away.

Health practitioners can channel the energy of this symbol while they work with a client, or invite their clients to gaze upon it before, during, or after a session to expand and accelerate healing potential.

Close your eyes, settle your mind, and breathe deeply as you prepare to harness the magical healing power of the universe. While feeling into your Heart, make an energetic connection with your recipient. Visualize the Teglih sigil while holding the recipient in your awareness, and request permission to use the healing power of Teglih for your subject's highest good. You will know that permission has been granted and the connection made when you feel a harmonic, subtle, yet distinct change in vibration.

Kahlsi

(Kel-si)

Respect, Honor, Love, Gratitude

Kahlsi encourages us to bring our integrity to a new level. It offers us an upgrade in our ability to love, honor, and respect ourselves and others. Our busy lives are filled with trials and troubles that can cause us to operate at less than our fullest capacity. It is common to conduct ourselves from less than our fullest integrity when under such life stressors. In order to live our best possible life, we need to tap into our brilliance, ground ourselves in Heart-centered awareness, and embrace our excellence each and every day.

Kahlsi shows us that we are all interconnected, and reminds us of how important our thoughts, feelings, and actions/reactions are—whether they are expressed or not. Our internal dialogue and our external actions are both connected to the Quantum Field, so nothing we do, think, or say is ever secret; everything is known on some level. Khalsi reminds us that everything we think and every action we take should come from the Heart and that our goal should always be to open to deeper states of Love, to inspire and uplift others, and to engage in life with creativity, clarity, and compassion.

Sit quietly with the symbol before you. You may wish to draw Khalsi on a separate sheet of paper or on a card. Light a candle and keep it nearby. Breathe deeply and slowly as you gaze upon the sigil. Be open to receiving Khalsi's upgrades of Love, respect, honor, and gratitude into your being for your highest good. When you feel the time is right, as you blow out your candle, say "I am open now to receiving upgrades of Love, respect, honor, and gratitude for my highest good, and for the highest good of all." Thank Kahlsi and the universe for their loving support and guidance.

Hydahama

(Hi-da-hahma)

Openness, Living in Harmony, Flow

Within each of us there exists a magically harmonious state. In this openness, we can live our lives in harmony and experience joy in our day-to-day activities. We can free ourselves from discord and work successfully with the challenges life so generously provides for our advancement. Hydahama reminds us that although life offers us many obstacles to overcome, it never serves us to be closed off in fear or hate. Hydahama tells us that by keeping an open Heart and an open mind, we can potentially adopt multiple different perspectives. By expressing compassion and truth in all our dealings, we can open up to infinite expansion of Self and find healing.

Our ego tries to build stories with false truths, adding to our confusion, pain, and suffering. These stories or beliefs are sometimes masked in a way that makes us feel better in the moment, but later on, guilt, shame, and blame take over and torture our minds. Hydahama holds an energy free from all confusion and resides in a place of Love where there is only *pure truth*. It gently shows us a quiet, centered, grounded place in which our emotions are still (but not silenced), the mind is at ease (but not numb), and the body is quiet (yet alert). We can experience all the chaos and complications of life but act in complete harmony with our environment and our higher selves.

73

When we are challenged, we have an opportunity to grow, to free ourselves from the chains we have acquired in our lifetimes. It is we who have forged and fashioned these chains and it is we who keep ourselves in bondage. How can we live in peace with ourselves and others when we carry weights that anchor us in our mundane existence? Hydahama's message is that it is time now to take responsibility for our life and our choices. We are infinitely powerful. We can heal and live a life of Love and liberty. It is possible. It is possible. It is possible!

You are capable. You are supported by beings of Love and Light, who stand ready to embrace you and answer your appeals. You need only to call upon them. You can free yourself from the limitations you yourself have imposed. Feel yourself expand…in clarity, in confidence, and in consciousness. Celebrate who you are!

Use this beautiful symbol, Hydahama, to assist you in moving through any challenges that arise when you take back your power and begin to resonate with the Love that you are. Sit quietly and calmly and close your eyes. Breathe deeply. Allow your mind to settle. Feel yourself sinking into the ground. Relax. When you are ready, open your eyes. Gaze upon Hydahama. Be open to receiving its direction and guidance. Still your mind and feel into the energies of this symbol. Feel the flow and harmony Hydahama emits. Intuitively draw its energies into your being. Stay with Hydahama until you feel your body resonate with its vital, vibrant energy.

Keep Hydahama close to you as a reminder of the direction in which you are headed: to a place within, peaceful, open, and free. What will you choose? A life of discord, shackled to your past? Or a life of harmony and freedom? Choose—and then get quiet and allow your choice to crystallize in your mind.

Bahan

(Ba-han)

Forgiveness

In this world of confusion and strife, many of us have left our Hearts behind. To flourish in this world requires forgiveness.

Forgiveness involves bringing forward your Infinite Love and stepping into a place of non-judgment towards self or other. True forgiveness is not about offering a forced, false feeling of superiority towards someone or something in order to make "amends." Instead, it is about coming to an understanding that an event occurred due to confusion. When we are grounded in who we are— beings of Love—we live from a place of appreciation and acceptance. We understand that when negative events occur, they occur in a space *outside* of Love. This is why we need to fill every situation in need of forgiveness with Light. This is not to say we relinquish our power or encourage negative events to occur. It simply means that when we find ourselves in a challenging situation, we bring ourselves back to our center, back to Love and Light.

To shed Light on any relationship or interaction, to smooth out difficulties and to heal fragmented energy, we need to tap into our integrity and draw our Love forward. This symbol, Bahan, shows us how to cut through confusion and cold-heartedness, find clarity, and bring Love into any difficult situation.

Sit quietly. Allow yourself to sink into the earth with every slow, deep breath. Close your eyes and calm your mind. When you are ready, think about a person (perhaps yourself) or event that is in need of your forgiveness. While thinking about this individual or circumstance, open your eyes and gaze softly upon Bahan. As you receive the knowledge and clarity Bahan is offering, allow the situation to soften. Let your emotions calm. Bahan offers to infuse this situation with Love. When you are ready, it will help you come to a state of ease, Love, and understanding. When you are finished, thank the situation for all it has taught you. Ask Bahan to help you release it from your being now. Once you feel the release is complete, thank Bahan for its loving guidance.

Halahma

(Hala-hma)

Finding Inner Fire, Strength, and Clarity
(Useful for Healing Abuse or Abuse of Substances,
and for Addiction Recovery)

Almost everyone today has addictive or abusive tendencies in one form or another. We are addicted to emotions, people, substances, foods, and activities. These addictions are often hidden in our subconscious minds. For those who have acknowledged their addictions and have brought them into the conscious mind, it can feel overwhelming, as though the addiction has a power that can never be overcome. Often, abuse and addiction go hand-in-hand. When we lose ourselves to abuse of any kind, we lose our sense of power. Halahma wishes to offer assistance in bringing forward our inner strength and clarity so we may take back our power and find the healing fire deep within.

Sit quietly and comfortably. There is no need with this practice to engage in any memories which may be triggering you. This is an exercise of softness and gentleness, stoking your inner fire so you may move through your healing process with greater ease. Breathe deeply. Relax

81

and sink into the earth. Gaze upon Halahma softly and notice the details of its lines, the way they flow. With your gaze remaining soft, open yourself to the warmth this symbol offers you now. Feel the warm glow in your lower abdomen, and feel the strength of the fire growing within.

With this new strength, be open to a change in your perception or motivation. You may find yourself choosing differently, in ways that are more in alignment with your authentic being. Refer to this symbol when you are in need of more fire, strength, and clarity in your life.

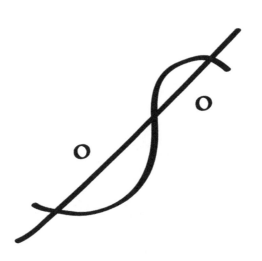

Khalagma

(Ka-lag-ma)

Releasing Mis-Qualified Energies, Removing Obstacles

Human beings have the potential to work with and master the powerful energies of Love, healing, and manifestation. What stands in the way of all that we wish to have in life are beliefs and energies, which we can actively choose to release, transmute, or clarify. If we want to live life freely, in happiness and ease, it is important to remove the obstacles (such as limiting beliefs) that we hold and place on ourselves.

You can work with this symbol, Khalagma, in many ways. You may choose to gaze upon it during meditation to help you tap into energies and beliefs which no longer serve you. You may choose to use it in art, or have a sacred ceremony with it during the full moon. Discover what feels best for you. Listen to your intuition—where does the symbol take you? Ask Khalagma to assist you in letting go of the thoughts and feelings you've picked up along the way which no longer serve you, freeing you to live more in alignment with your highest purpose.

As you work with this powerful symbol, you may find that shadow work is a natural next step. Shadows are manifestations of energies such as beliefs. They can take on many forms, but understand: no shadow that presents itself to you can bring you harm. Shadows are often stuck energies we picked up along our paths that served us in some way. However, as we heal, we need to release these patterns and beliefs, for they obstruct our authenticity and our Love.

Keep Khalagma before you as you relax your body and mind, preparing to release whatever shadows come forward. When you are settled and ready to begin, look at the symbol. Ask it to help you release energies that are ready to be released for your highest good. Ask for these energies to show themselves...and expect them to appear before you, in whatever form they present. You may ask if they have a message for you...or simply thank them for their service. Ask Khalagma to assist you in releasing the energies to the Light, where they will be transmuted, never to return. *See them go into the Light.* Then, ask Khalagma to help you bring in Light to fill the void that the shadow's departure has created. Feel yourself accepting the Light. Feel it filling you up. When you are finished, thank Khalagma for its assistance.

Hoitma

(Hoy-t-ma)

Cleansing Breath, Clearing Lungs

Breath revitalizes our entire body from our tissues to our cells, from our organs to our blood. It directly affects the action of our nervous system, and has the power to make us feel sick or well. When our breath is tight or restricted in some way, our lives are restricted. We lose our sense of freedom. Learning to breathe properly can have a direct and positive impact on our health—just as a loss of breath directly reduces the quality of our lives. If we have been experiencing a shortening of breath, it can take time to gain proper range and expansion again.

Hoitma suggests that it may be time to start a breathing practice, to free, mobilize, and expand your diaphragm and lungs. This symbol also carries a message that there may be something or someone in your life that is inhibiting your sense of freedom. If this is the case, this symbol holds positive energy for you to find a way to change this dynamic, to bring your life back into a state of greater freedom and balance. If you have lung or diaphragm issues, this symbol also offers healing to those areas in need.

To work with Hoitma's positive energy and the space it holds for freedom and balance, gaze upon the symbol softly while breathing as slowly and deeply as possible. Feel a sense of calm as you sink into the ground and feel the energies of Hoitma working to ease and expand your breath. Stay with this symbol for as long as you need to.

Pay attention to times when you catch yourself breathing in a shallow manner or holding your breath. Try to correct your breathing in these moments...you may choose to bring the energies of Hoitma to mind for support and guidance.

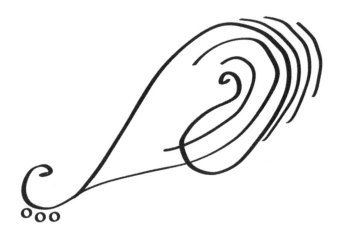

Dahanama

(Da-ha-na-ma)

Release Pain in the Physical Body

When the body is in pain, most often we want the pain to stop so we can get back to our lives. Even though pain is our body's way of communicating a problem that needs attention, there can be urgency or a dismissive quality to our thoughts and feelings. Some healers will advise us to go into the pain to try to understand what our body is telling us; others advise us to discover what eases the issue and to work directly with that. Dahanama meets us somewhere in the middle. Sometimes it is useful to become conscious of the story behind the pain; other times it is not. Engaging with this symbol's energy allows needed information to come to light in a way that is best for you, and helps to release your physical discomfort.

Sit down or lie down in whatever way is most comfortable for you, keeping Dahanama close by. Work on slowing your breath and releasing any tension or anxiety. Deepen your breath and close your eyes, calming yourself ever further. Feel a sense of sinking into the ground. When you have reached as calm a state as you can achieve today and you are ready to engage with Dahanama, imagine placing the symbol in the painful or tense area of your body. Breathe deeply and slowly for as long as feels appropriate.

You may use your finger to trace the lines of the symbol in this book. Draw it as you feel it...in every direction imaginable. There is no right or wrong way to trace Dahanama's lines, as experiencing different orientations will assist in the release of pain. Breathe slowly and deeply as you quietly trace the symbol with your finger. Allow its energies to help you release your pain. Even if you do not know what is happening in your body or why, Dahanama will work with you to support relieving your pain. If it is important for you to know the details of your dis-ease or discomfort, this information will come to you as you engage with the symbol, for this is what it is designed to do. Breathe, relax, and trace Dahanama with your finger for as long as feels right for you.

Go to Beauty and Peace

Go to Beauty and Peace

This eight-petaled flower is a reminder of how infinite we are, and that we are timeless. It reminds us of our wisdom, our experience, and our vast knowledge: all of us are eternal beings of Love, having temporarily forgotten who we really are. The sweetness that flows from this symbol is beautiful and peaceful; it reflects the beauty and peace within you. It abides in a place deep within all of us, in a place of stillness. It is a place we access in dreamtime, not far from waking consciousness.

There is softness all around us. There is beauty and grace even in the darkest corners of our being. This symbol reminds us to look for the peace within us as well as around us. We can experience the life we choose...a life full of Love and beauty.

Follow the lines of this symbol with your eyes or your finger. Each petal offers a different perspective; a new way to view your life and life circumstances. Observe the multiple directions, planes, and possibilities in which the petals point. See your circumstances from many different angles, in softness. Remember, this gentle symbol is showing you that beauty and peace exist within everything. What could you offer yourself within your life that would allow for more fulfillment and peace? Visualize your options as you trace the symbol with your eyes or finger. Then, apply your creative perspective to any areas in your life which cause you stress or concern—or use it in ways that will simply bring you more joy!

You may gaze upon this symbol any time you need assistance in observing a situation from multiple angles or you are in need of peace. Or, contemplate it before going to bed...it will remind you of where you are headed in dreamtime.

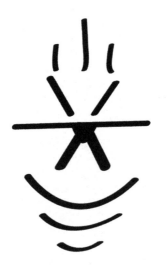

Pahma

(Pah-ma)

Love of the Highest Order

Simply gaze upon this symbol, Pahma, with an openness to receive. Pahma shows itself to you as a reminder that Love is within reach, that Love is all around you, and that Love is everywhere. You are Love. Pahma may be presenting itself to you as an offering from the universe, a means of support, gently guiding you back to Love. It may also be a message to be gentle with yourself and others, reminding you that we are all connected.

This symbol represents pure Love, as most of us have forgotten what Love actually is. Love heals all the energetic disturbances we carry within and around us, which cause various expressions of confusion, pain, and suffering. This symbol is a call to healing and a call of remembrance. It can help you to feel pure Love, and to feel reassured that there is a way to peace.

You may choose this symbol as a reminder of the quality of energy you choose to embody. Perhaps draw it on a piece of paper or a card and place it on your altar or in another special place. Keep it near you during your spiritual practices. Or, place it next to your bed or in your office space as a reminder to Be the Love that you are. You can meditate while softly gazing upon it, remaining open to feeling its frequency of Pure Love. Or, you can place a freshly-cleansed clear quartz crystal upon the symbol and ask for the frequency of Pahma to be activated within the crystal in its purest expression.

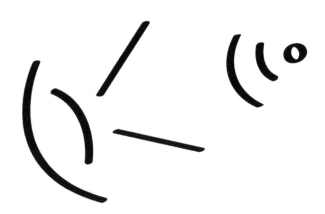

Lahma

(La-chh-ma - softly)

Non-Attachment, Letting Go, Freedom

A ttachment is a condition many of us are familiar with. If we are being honest with ourselves, we would admit to "majoring in it" for most of our lifetime! The skill of being able to let something go is only as challenging as we make it, and is dependent upon our emotional reactions and triggers. If we are feeling centered and balanced, we have a much easier time flowing with our lives and allowing situations to unfold. If we can find our centered place of peace and stillness, we feel light and free, with no attachments holding us back from living and experiencing what we deeply desire.

We can feel attached to a person, place, or thing, or we can be attached to an emotion, pattern, or behavior. Letting go is an art and a masterful skill. Lahma offers us assistance with the practice of non-attachment. It wishes you to understand that *non-attachment is a practice*. The more you work with the energies of letting go and staying unattached, the easier it will become, and the more easily you will navigate the seas of life.

First, we must be reminded of what it feels like to let go, and the lightness which arises through that release. We work hard to hold on to things: people, experiences, feelings, habits, etc. when in fact they no longer serve us. It's best to allow them to move on.

Sit quietly and comfortably, breathing slowly and deeply. Feel yourself settle into the ground. Gaze softly upon Lahma and ask the symbol to remind you what it feels like to be unattached; what it feels like to let go. Once you have experienced these feelings, call to mind something you are willing to release. Ask Lahma to assist you with this release for your highest good and for the highest good of all. Sit with this release until you feel a sense of lightness and freedom. Thank Lahma for its loving guidance.

Henama

(He-na-ma)

Healing Sexual Abuse and Trauma

Everyone, male or female, experiences at least one abusive or traumatic sexual event during their lifetime. Acting out in ways that lack respect towards ourselves and others is a sign of the times in which we live. In some family units, family members repeat ancestral patterns until one brave soul decides that "enough is enough" ... and takes on the responsibility of healing not only themselves, but also the relations who came before them and those who will come after them. For those willing to take on healing abuse and trauma, sexual or otherwise, the universe commends you for your courage, and stands with you in your process of acceptance, release, and empowerment. This is a noble healing, and is a solid step towards self-responsibility and taking back one's power.

The energy we carry within and around us is *attractive*: like attracts like. There is no sense carrying forward traumatic energy if you are actively choosing a life free from pain and suffering. It is time to release it and move forward, free to live from a joyous Heart.

Henama is a healing symbol of play and whimsy. Yet it is a symbol of integrity: it is strong, authoritative, and it disregards other's opinions when those opinions are not in full alignment with our Love. Working with this energy allows you to create a powerful space in which all events, creations, and relationships arise out of Love. Expressing yourself through creative outlets such as writing, painting, or dancing offers unique angles for healing trauma. This symbol may be used as inspiration in your creative endeavors, and when you use it in this way, the healing energies of Henama are amplified.

You may choose to sit quietly with this symbol and meditate, or bring it to other therapies as a support in your process. Henama wishes to share that you are never alone. It is time to be healed—you *are* healing, and you *will* heal. This symbol will assist you in healing all timelines and ancestral patterns of sexual abuse and trauma, no matter the magnitude.

Aman'kh

(A-monk)

Expression, Trust, Surrender, Freedom, Embrace Your Path

Surrender to your path. Trust in your path. Embrace your path. Feel free along your path, and don't forget to create along your path! Expressing ourselves is an important part of manifesting. We must be conscious of how we restrict ourselves, how we speak to ourselves and others, and we must trust our whole experience. If we are negative, or express ourselves in a negative way, our journey will reflect this in a less than optimal way.

Aman'kh is encouraging you to be expressive, to trust, and to embrace your path in happiness and joy. It is also reminding you to be conscious of your thoughts and actions as you walk through the world. Walk gently. Walk sweetly. Walk openly. Your participation on earth is celebrated and welcomed! Your unique gifts and talents are required and embraced! It is important that you express yourself as the Love that you are, and that you do not dim your Light. Trust in your process, and do your best to continue the process. There is much joy to be held by those who choose a positive path. It is a conscious choice, for every moment.

This symbol suggests it is time for a course correction. Notice what events, dynamics, or energies are occurring in your life, and ask yourself: "Is this truly what makes my Heart happy?" You are encouraged to surrender, trust, and embrace the journey you are on, even if it requires change. Trust your Heart, and beauty will arise through the chaos and confusion.

Jamaka

(Ja-ma-ka)

Centering, Moving through Overwhelm, Taking One Step at a Time

Life can be overwhelming and stressful at times. Many things—relationship upsets, job stress, or simply lack of sleep can make us feel ungrounded and as if we are out of control. When we feel a loss of control, it can be because we have lost our center and therefore have lost our power. Our center is our strength, our core. Ideally, we would choose to live and experience our life from this deep place of stability. During stressful times, often we need to slow down, take a deep breath, and take one step at a time. We need to move through the overwhelmed, anxious, intense emotional state and *soften.*

Jamaka encourages you to slow down, take one step at a time, and relax the energies around what burdens you. Gently let go of the pressures life presents, and instead, hold on to the knowing that everything is happening as it should. The outcome is always exactly as it needs to be...it can't be anything but perfect. The act of engaging with this symbol can remind you of where your center is located. It is never as far away as you think. Jamaka can teach you how to feel grounded, centered, light, and "in the flow." There is never a need for stress.

Take a moment for yourself. Try to let go of your worries. Gaze upon Jamaka and breathe, deeply and slowly. Notice the center of the circles, and breath their center into your own being. Notice the heaviness of the bottom circle and how it is supported lightly but firmly, grounding and anchoring the rest of the symbol. Feel into the lines as they express themselves, feel the lightness of the top part of the symbol. Remind yourself that you are capable. You are like this symbol.

Akuna

(A-ku-na)

Trusting Your Experience, Belonging

Oneness is a concept often spoken of in spiritual, religious, and metaphysical circles. It is a familiar word, but it can be challenging to understand its true meaning. We as seekers understand generally the concept of the connection between all things, and quantum physics has aided in the belief that one thing affects another through the phenomena engendered by entanglement. Unfortunately, we continue to try to understand these multidimensional realities of connectivity from the limited nature of our ego mind. In order to grasp the vastness and truly magical connection between all things, we must look with our Hearts, not our brains. We will never see truth without tapping into the infinite wisdom and connection of our Heart.

Akuna is about trust. It is about connecting with the eternal quantum field, wherein you are an individual expression of the whole. You *belong*. You belong everywhere with everything, and the role you play is equal to the person, plant, or animal standing next to you. Akuna wishes to bring forth your trust of the oneness within you. You know that all things are connected and you will find this connection in your Heart. Once again, we call forward the infinite wisdom of your Heart, trusting it to step above the ego mind and to express bravely the Love and connectivity it knows beyond measure.

You may choose to draw, chant, or gaze upon Akuna as you contemplate what oneness means to you. Place one or both hands on your Heart center to bring your attention there as you relax into your practice. Allow your Heart to show you what this symbol is attempting to teach you. You cannot go wrong. Your Heart is capable of showing you the truth about belonging and about trusting the uniquely beautiful expression of life you are creating on this planet.

Yunami

(Yu-na-mi)

Remember, Reflect, Gain Clarity, Make Connections

The human experience of loneliness is one we commonly share. Out of desperation, we cling to relationships as we attempt to mask the illusory pain of separation. At some point during our early development, most of us forget that we are always connected through what scientists now call the Quantum Field.

But how can we remember the feeling of being connected? How can we gain clarity about things beyond what we can perceive with our limited senses? How do we get to a place of remembrance, where we can contemplate our oneness and realize that truly, we are never alone?

Yunami is calling you forward, calling you to embrace a higher purpose. This symbol holds the frequency of making connections and finding clarity within these connections. It also suggests that you expand on your current spiritual practice, or, if you do not have a practice now, then to choose one that works for you. Yunami also suggests there are currently relationships in your life which are either out of balance or are no longer of service to you. If you are ready to let go of a relationship, now is a good time to do so, in gratitude for and in honor of all involved.

If we are too attached to someone, we will have a hard time embracing our authentic self, and will be less able to feel and embrace the interconnection of all. Yunami assists us in the process of releasing toxic relationships and connections.

Before working with this symbol, set your healing intensions clearly. For example, maybe you would like to let go of toxic or unbalanced relationships, gain clarity about past relationships, or remember universal oneness. Sit quietly. Breathe deeply with the symbol before you, feeling yourself sink into the ground. With soft eyes and your intentions set clearly in your mind, gaze upon Yunami. Ask the symbol to assist you with your healing in your highest good. Stay with this practice for as long as is appropriate for you.

Humbelah

(Hum-bel-ah)

Heart Full of Gratitude

One of the most pleasant and powerful feelings we can know is gratitude. Gratitude comes from our Heart; it is a variation of the frequency of Love. When we feel gratitude, our whole being lights up. We have greater coherence (an ability to think clearly from, and to resonate with, our Heart), a greater capacity to give and receive, and feelings of pleasure about life that are almost indescribable. But through our various traumas and life circumstances, gratitude can be lost. We can forget what its pure energy can feel like, and we can lose touch with our Hearts.

Humbelah embodies the infinite frequency of pure gratitude. Gratitude bursts from its every line and curve. If you haven't felt gratitude for a while, or if you struggle to feel it, this symbol will work with you to find it again. If you are acquainted with gratitude, Humbelah shares and amplifies this magical energy within you. We can never have too much gratitude! For those wishing to consciously manifest in their physical lives, gratitude is key. We must be thankful, not because we are pressured to do so, but because thankfulness radiates naturally from our Hearts.

For those who choose to bring forth a Heart full of gratitude, know that this also includes joy and delight! Hold the intention of embracing these natural energies and states of being. With your hand over your Heart center, gaze softly upon Humbelah. Breathe deeply. Feel yourself sink into the ground. Feel your Heart space beneath your hand. Allow your Heart to open as you look at the symbol, continuing to breathe slowly and deeply while sinking into the ground. Relax and release anything you may need to release. Ask to become more acquainted with gratitude. Remain with Humbelah for as long as you need to. You may wish also to draw this symbol on a nice piece of paper and have it somewhere you will see often, to reinforce keeping your Heart full of gratitude habitually.

Delight

Seeing Clearly, No Confusion:
Remembering Who We Are

Everyone we know (our friends, family, colleagues, our animal pals, even we ourselves) is living and experiencing life through a unique set of programs. These programs have served a purpose in our development. We can be grateful for them and for all they have taught us. However, as we strive for a state of clarity, there comes a time when it is in our highest good to release those programs that no longer serve us. Clarity means that we experience no confusion in our mental, emotional, physical, or spiritual bodies...at any level. Clarity is remembering and knowing ourselves: *the Love that we are.*

In order to be the Love that we are, we must let go of our own programs, which serve eventually to cause only suffering. Our programs are subconscious responses such as anger, fear, and pain—all are the misguided reactions of someone who has forgotten who they are. As we become more clear about who we are, as we remember the Love that we are, our confusion lifts. We see the world around us differently, as a place of beauty, as opposed to a painful, hostile place. When we begin to embrace the Love that we are, when we see truth rather than confusion, we access our power in a most excellent way. Suddenly, our intentions carry more weight. We start to see the results of our requests for a better, more fulfilling life. We become masterful in our manifestations. We experience the connection to All That Is, and our suffering is released.

This symbol, Delight, is calling upon you to remember who you are: a being of Love. It is time to embrace the Love that you are, fully and completely.

Congratulations! Delight brings you a powerful message, and though you may be confused as to how to progress, know that your path is unfolding before you perfectly. It's time to find your power and to embrace it as a being of love and beauty. Use the symbol Delight especially during a full or new moon to set the intention that you choose to seek truth—the truth within and the truth all around you.

Love is all around you! Use the following affirmations daily, and as part of a full moon or new moon ceremony:

"I choose to see clearly, no confusion."

"I am love."

"I embrace fully the love that I am."

Kahalula

(Ka-ha-lu-la)

The Love Felt Between Twin Souls

Many people are on a Twin Soul (Twin Flame) journey (a dance between two souls who hold a similar energetic signature). This is often a complicated and challenging road, filled with ups and downs, with what can feel like no end of lessons to be learned. Sometimes, during challenging moments or phases, we need a reminder of why we are enduring the levels of confusion, frustration, and (often) great heartache that is all too common with this chosen journey. Even if your Twin isn't incarnated, you can still work with the energies and lessons associated with Twin Souls.

Kahalula holds the frequency of the Love and completeness felt between Twin Souls or Twin Flames. The dance which occurs as Twins trigger each other can be confusing, as the triggers often represent opposites: attraction and repulsion; yearning and animosity; obsession and indifference. Yet Twins pursue one another…only to then avoid one another. One Twin will attach fully to a relationship, while the other can't run away fast enough! These are all opportunities for healing, to work through karmic lessons, and to integrate energies the soul has chosen to work with and advance through. It is a challenging dance, but a dance of beauty nonetheless.

Kahalula reminds you that the Twin relationship is one of great healing...for those willing to do the work. When you heal yourself, you heal the other person, and offer great healing to all Beings. Understand that the triggers are surfacing to be healed—and with a greater perspective can even be viewed with gratitude. Having a sense of gratitude can make the struggles between Twin Souls (or any soul relationship) less intense. Often, the triggers which surface in Twin relationships are potent because they are healing many layers at once. In other words, it's an efficient way to heal. Most likely, your soul—you—chose this path for this reason. It's important to understand that the more you process and release, the more enjoyable life becomes.

Sit with Kahalula when you are in need of support throughout your Twin journey. Remember, it is a dance. Do your best to heal the energies that come to the surface. Kahalula is offering love that is familiar to you: the love felt between you and your Twin. Gaze upon this symbol gently, in a calm, receptive state, and feel the Love connection.

Pahgyahma

(Pah-gyah-ma)

Healing with Earth and Sun Energy

This symbol assists us with merging Sun and Earth energies for both local and distance healing.

All life on our beautiful planet carries within it the frequencies of Mother Earth. We are all offspring of the Earth, and we resonate with her healing tones. The Earth is a divine feminine energy, providing the nurturing that all living beings require to thrive. The Sun is a powerful masculine life force, providing energy for life on our planet. The Sun and Earth make a powerful healing connection.

Pahgyahma is a symbol of healing, protection, life, uplifting emotions, and building energy. This symbol combines the energies of the Sun and Earth so that we may work with and integrate their healing properties with greater ease. Use this symbol to help connect you further to the energies of the Earth and the Sun. Work slowly. Pick one energy at a time to focus on. You can do this by meditating while gazing upon the small circle on the bottom of the symbol as representing the Earth. Conversely, to familiarize yourself with Solar energy, focus on the Sun at the top of the symbol. Once you are familiar with the feel of the Earth and Sun as individuals, gaze upon the symbol in its entirety to connect the two energies. This is a lovely and powerful energy to work with in support of healing anything that ails you. As noted, it can be used both locally and for long-distance healing.

Yahma

(Yah-ma)

Transfer of Energy

Every form of life, whether it is a human or a rock, has an individual 'energetic signature,' based upon the Love that it is. Every unique vibrational pattern holds information that the life form's soul wishes to express and share with the world. In the case of physical objects (such as crystals), we can find it helpful to move a particular energetic frequency from one object to another. This is most often done with physical objects we wish to enhance or adapt, so they will perform a certain task to assist us in some way. Yahma can be used to transfer frequencies from one object to another, assisting you in communicating across dimensions with angels, guides, or other Spirits of the Light you might wish to contact. Yahma can help you to access your channeling abilities, and serve as a conduit to bring forth and strengthen your unique gifts and talents and anchor them in your physical body.

To use this symbol for physical objects:
Cleanse both objects as appropriate. Place the object with the original energy you wish to transfer on the bottom half of the symbol, and place the object you wish to empower on the top half of the symbol. Then say, "I request that

the beneficial energies from (name the bottom object) be transferred wholly and completely in my highest good and in the highest good of all, to (name the top object). Thank you."

Although this energy exchange can occur instantly, leave the objects together for as long as you feel is necessary.

To use this symbol for yourself:

Sit quietly and comfortably, feeling as relaxed as possible. Take a moment to breathe deeply. Allow your mind to soften. Set your intention for working with Yahma, whether it be to enhance your communication with Spirit, angels, and guides, or to assist you with integrating an energy that will help you to improve your life in a most excellent way. Look deeply into the symbol, while holding your intention. Breathe deeply, as if you were breathing in the essence of the energy you are choosing to connect with. Stay in this relaxed space with the symbol as long as it feels right for you.

Hennami

(Hen-naa-mi)

Higher Communication, Connecting with Spirit/Beings, Being Protected by Light and the Highest Integrity

Everyone has available to them a group of Light Beings who are waiting to be called on for assistance. Many people want to communicate with Spirit, yet they are afraid—they haven't learned how to distinguish between a Spirit who comes in the Light and an energy of a darker nature. Hennami protects the integrity of communications with Light Beings so we can practice releasing the fear associated with communication. There is no need for fear, ever. For many of us, the belief of "fear" needs to be healed. Until this happens, we need assistance and reassurance that we are safe and protected.

It is possible to communicate with Light Beings when they are incarnated also. Hennami will work with the energies in the highest good of all, to ensure that you and the Beings of Light you wish to communicate with are held in a sacred space.

Before communicating with Spirit (incarnated or not), it is important that you take the time to set your intentions and to ground yourself in full honor and integrity. You may begin communications by asking Hennami to please protect the energies around you and the Being you wish to communicate with, in Love and Light, and with an interaction of ease. Hennami will help to facilitate accurate information, provided that you remain as clear, calm, and open to receiving as possible.

As you gaze upon the symbol, do your best to envision and feel Spirit. To initiate interaction, ask some simple questions. Working with simple questions in the beginning will help to establish a clearer line of communication so you can have a discussion which carries more emotional connection for you. Always finish these conversations by thanking the Spirit you were speaking with, and thank the energies of Hennami for facilitating and protecting the sacred space. It is also a good practice to offer blessings and gratitude for all involved.

Gyla

(Gai-la)

Coming to Fruition, Growth, Expansion, Development, Creation, and Creativity

We all walk a path unique to us. We all make unique choices, learn in unique ways, and integrate our lessons in a way that is unique to us. Once we begin to understand that we aren't being punished by life's happenings, and that experiences are for learning and growing, we can shift our perspective. We can see our experiences with gratitude, even the challenging ones. We can see the beauty and opportunity all around us. We can understand that Karma is our interaction with self-and-other, expressed through lessons for the purposes of growth, expansion, and development, rather than as a score card of "good" and "bad." With this understanding, there is room for us to release our fears and embrace our infinite capacity for Love and creativity.

Gyla stands for power, grace, and softness as you expand into knowing yourself as a radiant soul. It shows you a beautiful way to walk your path, a way of knowing that all the pieces of your life are falling into place. Gyla asks you to trust the process, to trust the Divine, and to trust yourself. This symbol serves as a reminder to look within, to know your resplendent Self. It reminds us not to take our lessons so seriously. There can be a sense of lightness and playfulness as we learn and experience.

If you require assistance in accessing greater levels of creativity or creation, you may use this symbol as part of your meditation practice. Gyla may also be used to assist you in any growth, expansion, or development you may seek. With your eyes softened, gently gaze upon Gyla. Trust the creative flow—it is natural for you at this time to open up to your creativity once more.

Kahli

(Kah-li)

Karma

In order to bring more of our true self forward, healing must occur in our past, present, and future, on all levels in time and space. We do not always need to know the reasons or the stories behind why we "are the way we are," particularly when investigating past lifetimes, however interesting they may be. Sometimes it is helpful simply to allow the healings to occur, with little disruption to our physical, mental, and emotional bodies. Simply heal!

Kahli helps us to learn from our emotions, our interactions with others, and our experiences. It helps us to neutralize the energetic charge within our lessons and to dissolve karmic ties when we have completed our lessons with others. Take note, however…even though we may believe we have completed our karmic dance with someone, this symbol will not dissolve karmic ties if our soul chooses to engage with someone further. It will, however, send a message to your soul that your incarnated aspect, your lower self, wants to make a different choice. This may well have an impact on the outcome of a situation—as long as it's in your highest good and in the highest good of all.

From our soul's perspective, everything we do and experience is for our soul's advancement. Our choices, reactions, and interactions define our karma. We get tangled up in situations, just to learn how to get untangled, so we can tangle up with something else. Some may call these lessons "mistakes," but from our soul's vantage point, they are simply glorious opportunities to learn and grow!

Kahli takes you on a journey of releasing karma that is ready and able to be released. Karma is not about "good" or "bad." It is about *learning*. Are you hanging onto any karmic lessons? Are you ready to let them go? Sit quietly, breathing slowly and deeply. Allow yourself to sink into the ground and quiet your mind. Gaze upon Kahli with soft eyes, as you continue to breathe slowly and relax further into the ground. Bring a situation into your mind, and play through the memory once. Then, with the memory fresh in your mind, allow yourself to be drawn into Kahli's spiral, feeling the support and containment of the four directions which border it. Gently ask Kahli to help you release this energy now, for your highest good and for the highest good of all. When your healing is complete, thank Kahli for its assistance. You may work with Kahli as often as needed.

Ughma

(Ugg-ma)

Connection to Soul, Soul Retrieval, Authentic Self

On the deepest of levels, so many of us feel lost. From the time we are small children, we accumulate illusions, false beliefs, and traumas, and all take us further away from who we are as our authentic self. Ughma can show us pieces of our authentic self by creating a portal to a place where we can recall and regard the purity of our soul. We are given an opportunity to remember who we are, and begin the journey back from feeling lost to feeling at home within ourselves.

Ughma shows us how we can reclaim our authenticity, through truth, trust, and integration. We are whole. We have been whole always. We release that which does not belong to us. We release lack of Love. We integrate the pieces of our Love that have become fragmented through our experiences.

Remember, Love is who we are...who we all are. Love is our authentic self, and Love defines us, through a frequency we express individually. The more of our Love we can bring forth and shine outward into the world, by owning our distinctive gifts and talents, the more we are authentically whole. We express ourselves more fully and completely by being the Love that we are.

Sit with Ughma before you while you settle your mind and relax your body. Slow and deepen your breath and allow yourself to sink into the ground. When you are ready, gaze upon Ughma with soft eyes, allow its message to penetrate your being. It will offer to take you on a journey to recall pieces of yourself you thought you had lost. You won't need to go far, as the pieces will show themselves in perfect timing. Do not worry if you feel you haven't made a connection with the "lost" pieces of yourself. This process happens on many levels—of which time is a part—so there is no need to rush. Take a deep breath. Welcome any aspects of the Love that you are to express themselves at this time. When you have finished, gently thank Ughma for this healing. Ask Ughma to help you to continue integrating the Love that you are. Meditate with Ughma whenever you are in need of assistance in either assimilating fragments of yourself or deepening your connection to your soul.

Suri

(Tsu-ri)

Enlightenment

In our modern world, many of us feel obliged to conform to societal pressures through means such as our career choice, our outward appearance, even our relationship choices. Some of our "choices" haven't been in full alignment with our Hearts, and inevitably, they cause upset to some degree. Society's pressures make it challenging for us to learn about what really makes us happy, and external demands can encourage us to neglect the very essence of our being. As a result, we can drift away from our truth, our Love, our center, and become engrossed in our ego self.

Attaining enlightenment means that we need to let go of appearances and societal pressures in order to create greater space within ourselves for more Light, Wisdom, and Love. Enlightenment, in part, is about letting go of all expectation, illusions, and our ego. As we move towards the stillpoint within ourselves, we reach out of our falsities, out of our ego-self, out of illusion, and into the peaceful collective consciousness of All That Is. We find forgiveness. We find grace. Enlightenment is a journey of gathering—and becoming—more Light. It is the joy of the exploration to find that sweet place, free from external pressures and stressors.

Enjoy the search! It is meant to be fun! Close your eyes and imagine what it might feel like to be in a space that is soft, free from worldly pressures...a place that feels light, where your mind needs no words because there is simply *knowingness*. Imagine that you could reach this place with ease. Know it is possible...it is within you.

Suri wishes to help ease the struggles that dim your Light, so you may begin to gather more Light. Suri emits an anchoring and grounded energy. It holds a space to help us reach beyond our limited senses to the still place deep within ourselves. It is a place of pure Light and joy, where all is understood and all is accepted.

With your eyes closed, sit quietly and comfortably. Breathe deeply and allow yourself to sink into the ground. When your mind is quiet and you feel relaxed, open your eyes and gaze upon Suri. Feel yourself anchored to the earth, held in her loving embrace, as Suri takes you on a quiet journey, gathering Light. As you look at this joyous symbol, feel into your Heart space. Feel yourself expand in all directions. Notice that there is a density to your expansion...you may not have felt this sensation before. Is there a slight difference in the quality of the energy as you expand? Feel into your six directions—front-body, side-bodies, back-body, into the ground, and out the top of your head. Work with Suri for as long as you need to, and when you are finished, thank Suri for its assistance in helping you bring more Light into your being.

Commagt

(Com-ma-gt)

Releasing Confusion

Confusion blocks our ability to see clearly, and encourages a life of struggle. When we are confused, we create false stories and draw conclusions that are not in alignment with our Heart.

In our modern society, it is normal for us to feel confused—confusion is accepted, promoted, even encouraged. Anger and frustration can grow within us throughout our lives because confusion restricts our access to our Heart, and limits our authenticity. It keeps our thoughts small, so we feel fear. Commagt helps us to release the stories we hold in our conscious ego mind, whether it be confusion about relationships, jobs, or situations (or even bigger confusions such as the interconnectivity of all things: oneness). As we release our stories of confusion, we gain freedom and insight...and we embody more of our authentic self. Our Love expands, and we have more clarity for all that is most important to us, both as individuals and collectively.

As you contemplate the confusion you experience in your life, notice the potential for release shown in the drawing of Commagt. Without diminishing its importance to you, consider whether or not this story, this confusion, is something you want to carry with you throughout your life...or if it is story you wish to release.

Close your eyes and place one or both of your hands over your Heart center. Breathe slowly and deeply, feeling into your Heart. When you are ready, ask your Heart to come forward with its wisdom, compassion, and understanding for this story. If you are in need of assistance, you may notice with your inner vision that a woman dressed in white appears. This is the Ascended Master and Divine Mother of compassion and grace, Kuan Yin, gently offering to guide you. Ask your Heart to show you the truth of the situation which has been upsetting you. Be patient. This truth may come to you over a couple of weeks, or you may know the truth immediately. This is a step towards your Heart breaking free of confusion. Practice checking in with your Heart often. Soon your Heart will become a natural place of calm, harmonious existence.

Zahay'kma

(Za-hay - kma)

Forgiving Self

How we react and recover from stressors depends upon our soul's mission, and how much healing we've done. Every situation, regardless of our "positive" or "negative" perception of it, has a positive intent. The positive intent is the learning opportunity provided through our experiences (our lessons) so we can advance as souls. Just as an innocent child learns that it hurts to touch a hot element on a stove, we all make (what we believe to be) mistakes so we can learn. These mistakes do not require our condemnation. They do not make us evil, or sinners in need of endless punishment. We are all, on a soul level, beautiful, innocent Divine Beings of Light learning to navigate situations meant to challenge us.

Forgiveness of self and "other" becomes extremely important along our healing journey—it doesn't serve us to punish further that which never should have been punished in the first place.

Forgiveness means seeing self and other as Divine Beings of Love; knowing that we and "the other" are fellow travellers, bumping along on a karmic path of growth and self-discovery. Forgiveness lies in remembering the innocence and beauty of self and other by releasing the confused, misguided expressions we mistakenly perceive and judge as errors. Once we are able to find the positive intent within a situation, we are more easily able to let go of the energies which caused our dis-ease and create space to grow and expand.

Sit quietly and comfortably, with Zahay'kma before you. Call to mind an event or person you wish to forgive. You may even wish to forgive yourself for something. Consider the positive intent of the circumstances surrounding that which you choose to forgive. No matter how challenging or triggering an event may be (or may have been) for you, there is always a positive intent. See beyond the illusion of darkness and confusion, and envision Light surrounding the situation, person, or yourself. Once you have found the positive aspects, remember that you are a Divine Being of Light, and that the circumstance before you is simply a lesson for which you have just found positive reasoning. Here is a place in which you have found forgiveness.

Anami

(A-na-mi)

Finding and Developing Self-Love

Egoless Love of Self can be elusive for many people. Somewhere along the way, it was misplaced, forgotten, hidden, or suppressed. Now, when we want it back, we can't remember where we put it. "It can't have gone far!" we exclaim. Like losing the keys to our home, losing Self-Love is uncomfortable; it causes tremendous upset and distress. Fortunately, Love hasn't gone far. It is still within us, like a hidden treasure. To locate it, we need to act. Our actions of Self-Love will begin the process of bringing our Love forward once again. We must be conscious of our thoughts, behaviors, and actions. "What am I thinking?" "What am I saying?" "What am I doing?" Be aware of the answers to these questions. Ask yourself, "Would Love do this?" If the answer is "No," then whatever you are doing is not conducive to finding your Love. Self-Love is connection, consciousness, and action from the Heart. It feels limitless—it is a joy so full that all of our needs are met. It is sweet and soft, yet powerful and confident.

It is important not to mistake Self-Love for arrogance. Arrogance is the ego, acting without direction from the Heart.

Sit quietly and relax. Breathe deeply and gaze upon Anami, which wishes to connect you deeply with your Heart. As you place one or both of your hands over your Heart center, set the intention to work with the beautiful energies of Anami. With each inhalation, allow the energies to wash over you, growing with soft intensity. Take them in. Feel a solidity with the energies as they grow. Sit with Anami for as long as you feel is right for you. Drawing this symbol on a card or on a nice piece of paper and placing it on your altar (or somewhere you will see it often) can help you to find, develop, and embrace Self-Love.

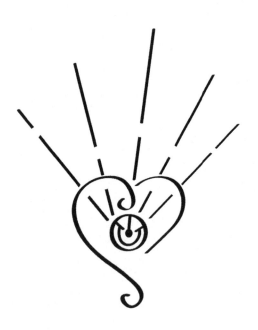

The Love That You Are

Self-Love, Knowing One's Worth, Expression of Self

We recognize one another by the signature of our Love. Everyone has a signature unique to them, which describes one's individuality within the whole. This symbol helps us to find and feel the Love that we are, and to find a stronger, more connected and integrated expression of who we are.

Allow yourself fifteen to twenty minutes to sit quietly with this symbol. When you are ready, place your hand on your Heart center...this helps you to connect to the Heart space within you. Relax and breathe deeply, sinking into the earth. Gaze softly at the symbol. Allow your Heart to expand, radiating out into space. There are no judgments, only expressions of love, the Love that you are. You are unique and beautiful, a light for the world to see and embrace. Feel your beauty and grace emanating from your Heart center as you gaze upon the symbol and allow it to assist you in remembering who you truly are.

Jyak'ma

(Yak-ma)

Self-Reflection, Self-Discovery, Self-Exploration

Welcome! Jyak'ma is about deeply knowing ourselves...exploring, discovering, and reflecting upon who we are; embracing who we are; engaging with all of our gifts so we can participate in the world with self-awareness! What fun this process of discovery is! Every single person has unique and wonderful talents, but to share them fully in the best possible way, it behooves us to know who we are. Our own particularities: our unique reactions, triggers, likes, and dislikes, are simply the "masks" we wear as Divine Beings of Light. We all come from pure, loving Source energy, with a unique signature or signal which defines our Love. When we incarnated on Earth, we chose to interact with and learn from certain karma and energies. The personality we incarnate with and develop throughout our life is the "mask" we wear in this lifetime. Our souls chose to bring forth a particular array of talents to contribute to the world. Our souls also chose to embrace a particular set of challenges expressed through various personal traits and karmic ties. Life is like acting in a wonderful (and sometimes challenging) play, in which we are given the opportunity to act out our roles for the purpose of growth and expansion.

Jyak'ma encourages you to have fun in the process of getting to know yourself.

Sit quietly and get comfortable. Allow your eyes to soften as you gaze deeply into this symbol. Feel the multidimensional aspects of Jyak'ma. Know that you are much more than a human being. While you explore Jyak'ma, draw in any information or feelings which arise. The energies are helping to reveal your distinctive qualities of Light and beauty. Allow Jyak'ma to guide you on your journey of self-discovery—wonderful, illuminating worlds lie ahead. Enjoy the process!

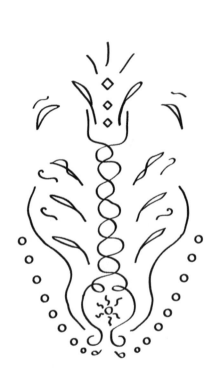

Galagma

(Ga-laa-g-ma)

Love from Within, Kundalini Energy

Kundalini energy is a life-force energy, and the core essence of personal power. It is our fire…and it is suppressed in many of us. When it flows properly throughout the body, it starts at the base of our spine, moving upwards, engaging with and activating the entire chakra system. When it flows naturally, we notice an increase of energy, an expansion of our intuition and psychic abilities, and it brings us a greater sense of peace and connection to all things. Kundalini energy is our Love. Galagma symbolizes and holds the frequencies of our Love, flowing beautifully throughout our body in a most excellent way.

In order to open the channels throughout our body so kundalini energy can flow with ease, we need to continue our healing process. We can work to increase our capacity to hold Love and Light, and to augment our body's ability to allow energy to move and flow through and around it. Our bodies need to be reminded of how to do this efficiently. While we do our good spiritual practices, healing our past and current traumas, we can also work towards increasing our capacity to hold and work with our energy bodies. The more energy we carry, and the more mastery we can embrace with that energy, the more adaptable we are—we don't lose ourselves in emotions or traumas, or in events that normally would displease or upset us. We can maintain calm and peace, even during challenges.

Galagma invites you to call forth your excellence. You are a Divine Being of Love, with no limitations other than those you impose upon yourself. It is time to embrace the Love that you are, and to engage with the natural flow of energy within and around you. This symbol encourages you to continue exploring and developing your spiritual practice. This might include meditating, writing, yoga, or a change in diet…anything that calms and centers you and actively engages the divine within you. Galagma wishes to remind you that you are never alone. You are always connected to the All, and the beings of Light that love and support you are waiting to step in and guide you— you need only ask.

Tungah

(Tung-ah)

Aligning with Information

Often, throughout our exploration of Self, we need new thoughts, ideas, or concepts introduced to us in different ways...such as through teachers or various forms of media. Everyone has a unique way of learning, a chosen preference in language and delivery with which they resonate most easily. This symbol, Tungah, helps us to take any concept we are struggling with understanding, learning, or integrating, and assists us in bridging the gap. It can help us to remove blocks we may hold, to move past a language barrier, or to be open to receiving new information.

To work with this symbol, begin with your simple meditation practice. When you feel grounded, calm, and open to receive, gently focus your eyes upon Tungah. Ask Tungah to assist you in being open to learning and assimilating information new and old with greater ease now. Continue to breathe slowly and deeply, feel yourself opening to new possibilities of understanding and integration. When you are ready, thank Tungah for its assistance, and show yourself gratitude for your willingness to grow and expand!

You may also choose to draw this symbol on a special piece of paper or take a picture of it so that you may look at it when you feel yourself struggling to understand or integrate something into your being.

Kalak'tuk

(Ka-lak-tuk)

Integrating Dimensions, Moving through Dimensions, Collapsing Time

Somewhere along our journey, it can be fun to explore and work within various dimensions. Every time we meditate, for example, we enter a space that feels different from the one we were in when we first sat down. Why? Because we have crossed into an alternate dimension! Even our dreamtime is spent in a dimension other than where our waking consciousness resides.

Just as we can move through dimensions, it is possible for us to work with time in a way that by today's standards and society's agreed-upon limitations is considered uncommon. Physicists have established that time—as we have come to know it—is not a fixed construct. Every time we gaze at the stars, for example, we are looking back in time, for the light we see is millions of years old. It is even possible that the star we are looking at no longer exists!

It can be an expansion of self to contemplate time. What is time? How do I relate to it? How does it affect me? This symbol, Kalak'tuk, introduces the idea that we human beings have the capacity to work with time in a more masterful way. Why take years or lifetimes to heal, for example, when we could collapse time and heal in days, hours, or minutes? Kalak'tuk is showing us this potential, opening our awareness to this reality.

To work with this symbol, begin with your simple meditation practice. When you feel grounded, calm, and open to receive, gently focus your eyes upon Kalak'tuk. Feel yourself opening to the information it wishes to share with you. Look or feel into its lines and curves, and sense the unlimited nature and promise of this multidimensional symbol...you can move past the constraints of time and space, and merge with the oneness that exists in non-time, in infinity. When you are finished, thank Kalak'tuk for its assistance today. You may work with this symbol as often as you like, especially if you have become consumed with your life and need help in once again seeing the bigger picture.

Lakama

(La-ka-ma)

Turning Outward Beauty into Inner Beauty

Many of us are guilty of projecting our desire for Love upon someone or something other than ourselves. We hope that actively loving another person will relieve the pain of not loving ourselves. Unfortunately, if we love something outside of ourselves and hold a belief in separation, this love we feel is not Love; it is something else. It is not Love because there are strings attached. When we feel lack, we are not full of our Love. If we are not full, we tend to grasp whatever false illusion will make us believe we are full. Regardless of the reasons one lacks Self-Love (which can be numerous, both individually and collectively), we have the choice to work through the illusory barriers which keep us from being the Love that we are. When we *are* full of our Love, and we love another, there are no needs, wants, or expectations. We allow the other to be free, and we honor them.

To work with this symbol most effectively is a two-part process. To begin, write a list of traits, gifts, talents, and qualities that you believe are positive aspects which describe you. On a separate piece of paper, write a list of all the negative traits and qualities you believe to be true about yourself. Set up a safe place where you can burn the paper on which you have written your "negative" traits. Have a glass receptacle on hand in which you can place the burning paper, and bring a jug of water along to put out the fire after burning.

So, for this exercise, you will need a lit candle, a firesafe container, a jug of water, your negative and positive belief lists, and the symbol, Lakama, either in this book or drawn on a separate piece of paper. You might consider bringing along a picture or video clip which will inspire in you a sense of gratitude or love as well.

In a space where you can safely light a fire, sit quietly with Lakama, and place your lists before you. Use common fire safety sense. Ask Lakama to help you to safely release with ease any and all beliefs you hold that prevent you from embracing the Love that you are in your highest good. Taking up your candle, carefully touch the flame to the paper containing your "negative" list. Place the burning paper in the glass receptacle, and as it burns, hold the intention and knowledge that you are letting go of the beliefs that hold you back. Allow yourself to feel gratitude for the teachings these beliefs have brought you. Once the fire has consumed the paper, thank Lakama for its assistance. Pour the water over the ash and set it aside so you can dispose of it respectfully and appropriately later.

Next, look upon your "positive" list and bring in a sense of love or gratitude, knowing you have released energies from your "negative" list. If you need assistance in creating this feeling, think of a person or event, or look at the picture or video clip. Once you are holding the feeling of love or gratitude within you, look at Lakama and ask it to help you bring forward, as the Love that you are, the list of positive traits you wish to embrace more fully and completely now. Read through the list, holding on to the beautiful energies, and allow them to swell within you as you read your list. When you are ready, ask Lakama to show you and help you to integrate all the amazing gifts and talents which have yet to present themselves to you. Ask for assistance in becoming, embracing, and living as the Love that you are. When this feels complete for you, thank Lakama for its assistance.

You may choose to keep your positive list of traits somewhere visible in your home as a reminder of your beauty and what you offer to the world. You can add to this list at any time, as you become more aware and accepting of your Love. You are magnificent! You deserve to hold this knowing in every cell of your being.

Shizama

(Shi-za-ma)

Releasing Negative Energy Space

When a thought or belief is anchored within us, it holds a specific vibration or frequency. This vibration attracts "like vibrations." For example, if you are feeling good one day, you might notice that people are particularly friendly or helpful, the perfect parking spot arises, and the thing you really wanted at the store is on sale. If you feel angry or upset, on the other hand, you might find that traffic is challenging, the dog won't stop whining, and everything is running behind schedule, creating havoc. These are superficial examples, but in reality, the attractive nature (like attracts like) of our thoughts and beliefs becomes the narrative of our life stories. Our thoughts and beliefs create our lives.

This is, after all, *your* life. Regardless of what you may believe or have been told, you are solely responsible for its outcome. This may feel daunting or overwhelming, but there is no reason to worry or to be fearful. You *can* take back your power, heal your wounds, and create the life you want. You don't have to continue down a path of victimization, repeating traumas and illness. You can choose to release all the negative energy space within and around you so you no longer attract negative energy! You can fill yourself with Light and become an attractor-field for all the wonderful things you want to have and to become!

This symbol works in two ways to assist us in releasing negative energy space. We need to make sure our homes are free of lower vibrational energy so our environment will help us in our healing journey. Shizama will help you to release negative energy within and around you.

For this exercise, you will need three lit candles. If possible, do this practice during or close to the full moon for maximum benefit, especially if you haven't cleared your living space previously. Place the candles a safe distance away from you, arranging them in a triangle around you, so you are sitting in the middle. Again, please use common fire safety sense.

With Shizama before you as you sit inside the triangle, light the candles around you in a clockwise sequence, while asking Shizama to help you to release from your living space all energies that are not of the Light. Once all the candles are lit, ask Shizama to release any and all negative energy from your living space now, for your highest good, never to return. Visualize all of the negative energy leaving, with the energies of Shizama ushering them out. The triangle you are sitting in will keep you protected from any resistant energies wishing to stay. When this exercise feels complete, Shizama will help you to create a barrier around your home, preventing lower vibrations from entering. Say aloud that you no longer welcome energies that are not in full, loving support of you on your path of Light, and that all energies that are not of the Light are no longer welcome and must leave.

Say this with authority, remembering that you are being assisted and protected.

Once you feel that the expulsion is complete, ask Shizama to help you clear any negative energy within or around you which is ready, willing, and able to be released in your highest good. Feel yourself becoming lighter as the heavier energy is transmuted, leaving your body and energy field. Once this process feels complete, ask Shizama to assist you in filling your home and entire being with pure white light. Close your eyes. Visualize and feel the amazing energy surrounding and filling you now. Stay with this filling process as long as you wish.

When you are done, thank Shizama for its help and protection. You may choose to do this practice as often as necessary. Use your intuition to decide how often is appropriate for you.

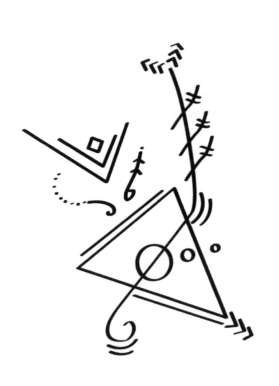

Jayagk

(Jai-yack)

Release Toxins on All Levels

The longer we live on our planet, the more toxins that accumulate in various levels of our mental, emotional, and physical bodies. Inevitably, these toxins have an undesirable impact. Toxins distort. Truth becomes misplaced. An energy which vibrates outside the domain of the Love that we are gains a foothold.

We gather and store toxins from the food we eat, the air we breathe, the fluids we drink, and the places and relationships with which we interact. What would it be like to be free of them? What would our sleep be like? Our digestion? Our ability to regenerate healthy tissues and organs? Because like attracts like, the more toxic we become, the more toxic we become.

In order to clear ourselves of toxins on all levels, we need to become more aware, *more conscious* of the areas within our lives that appear to be attracting toxins. Once we become and act with more awareness, clearing and shifting toxic energies and habits will help us dramatically to return to our authentic state. We will become even *more* conscious! We don't need to change our entire lifestyle (although some will choose this path because lifestyle is a controllable factor...some people feel comfortable adjusting to serve their needs). The consciousness we embrace will assist us in knowing what doesn't serve us in the best possible way. Take notice of the physical, emotional, and mental responses you have towards food, people, and the media, and ask yourself, "Is this a feeling and reality I want to develop further?" If the answer is "No," you need to make a change.

Use this symbol while contemplating and meditating on the toxic energies and situations in your life. Make the clear choice to release toxins from your entire being, while requesting assistance from Jayagk. With clear intentions, feel and envision the release and transmutation of the energies you no longer choose to carry forward and manifest. Stay with the releasing process as long as you feel is appropriate. Once it is complete, ask Jayagk to help you fill in the spaces with Light. Feel the warmth and purity of the Light, and thank Jayagk for its assistance.

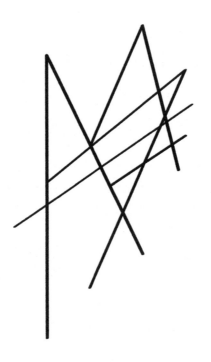

Panma

(Pan-ma)

Moving with Light, Expanding Frequencies

As we progress along a path of Light towards Light, we are able to hold a greater range of Light frequencies. Panma resembles how Light reflects and refracts. It shows us a greater spectrum of Light frequency, far beyond that which we can perceive with our physical eyes. Light is not limited to dimensions, only to the illusions we place upon it. Panma wishes to expand our ability to hold more Light in a greater range of frequencies. Panma shows us how to move with Light, dancing and playing in unlimited joy.

For the most part, we experience life through a Newtonian perspective of matter and gravity. This is an accepted truth in physics, but it doesn't explain everything we know or experience. As science evolves, it slowly confirms what people can experience when they are open to incredible, seemingly mind-bending possibilities.

Quantum physics has explained that light behaves both as a particle and as a wave. If we take this truth one step further, into our own spiritual experience, we can also have feelings differentiating between being a particle and a wave. When we live life as a particle, we are hard, resistant to change, bumping into struggles. When we move as a wave, we are fluid, light, and dynamic, able to bend and move in softness. The more wave-like we become, the greater the range of Light frequency we are able to hold. The greater our capacity to hold a range of frequencies, the greater our ability to adapt to the challenges life presents.

To work with this symbol, we must be ready to choose to become more Light. There is no downside, only the opportunity for easing pain and suffering. If you want to continue a life of pain and suffering, this symbol is not for you. For those who want to release limiting beliefs, however, Panma is honored to serve.

Sit quietly, breathing deeply, allowing yourself to sink into the ground. Gaze softly upon Panma as you continue to relax. When you are ready, ask Panma to help you open up to a greater spectrum of Light. Say aloud that it is your desire and intention now to hold greater frequencies of Light in your highest good. Sit with Panma. Allow it to take you where you need to go today. Do not be concerned if you can't see or feel changes, simply understand that the symbol is working with you on the levels most appropriate for you.

As you work with Panma, you may find shadows presenting themselves to be cleared. Simply thank the shadows for their service. Tell them it is time for them to go; that they are no longer needed. With clear intention, send them to the Light with blessings, never to return. Then ask Panma to fill you with Light, including the places where the shadows were residing. Feel yourself filling with Light.

When you are finished, thank Panma for its guidance. Ask it to continue working with you in your highest good. You may work with this symbol as often as you like.

Kalimar

(Kal-i-mar)

Divine Unity, Soul Family

As we've talked about before, separation and loneliness are common human experiences. Many of us are driven with an intense desire to fill the emptiness, often with another person or animal. We mistake general attachments to things outside ourselves for feelings of Self-Love and oneness, which is our true desire. We then find ourselves disappointed when what we truly seek remains beyond our reach. This is because the belief we still hold is the belief that separation is a truth; that we are separated from our Love and separated from one another.

It can be difficult to let go of a job, relationship, belief, or even a false reality before we are forced to. Many of us spend weeks, months, or even years clinging to something that we should have set free long ago. To our ego mind, it can be frightening to let go of what has been made obvious, drilled into us as truth. Or perhaps we want to hold on to something to convince ourselves it belongs to us, when it was never ours to begin with.

Ask yourself, "Am I willing to give up the illusion of separation and lack of Love?" It may seem strange that we would choose to hold on to suffering, but many of us do. It's what we know. Although it's become a part of us, it isn't who we are. Remember, we are Divine Beings of Love, always full of Light, always connected to everyone and everything. As long as we experience attachment, we will experience separation and lack. We will be unable to feel divine unity and our connection to our soul family. Wouldn't it be easier (and kinder) not to be attached? You have the ability to release *all* attachments. You are that *powerful*.

Kalimar holds the frequency for oneness and soul family connection but it is not simply handing it to us. We must learn to find this frequency without attachment. Kalimar will help us in learning how to let go of that which doesn't belong to us, freeing that which does belong to us, and allowing it to come forward. In this way, we may come to understand that the more we surrender, the more divine unity we feel.

Sit quietly and comfortably with Kalimar before you. Breathe deeply and slowly, allowing yourself to sink into the ground as your mind and body calms. When you are ready, gaze upon Kalimar with soft eyes. Continue to breathe slowly, staying as relaxed as possible. Kalimar will gently link with you in stages, in whatever way is appropriate. This process is not to be forced or rushed. Allow Kalimar to bring forward energies of oneness and connection. Let go of your fear, separation, and lack of Love. Trust the process. When you are finished, thank Kalimar for its assistance. You may work with this symbol as often as is appropriate for you.

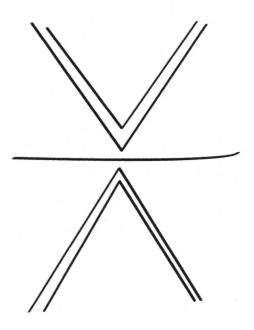

I AM Presence

I am the Consciousness of I AM

We are complete on all levels, at all times. I AM. We are infinitely loving and infinitely intelligent. I AM. We are capable of tapping into the universal fabric of consciousness, of oneness, where all of our needs are always met, where we are embraced, supported, and honored as a piece of the whole. Everything we could ever require is here for us, through the consciousness of I AM.

Our souls seek to grow and expand. Testing and exploring, we have a desire to discover, in lightness and joy. We dance and play through experience, through living life however it is presented to us. We do our inner healing work so we may find ease within our life's lessons, healing our fears, and embracing our infinite and limitless Love. I AM. The I AM Presence is who we are: whole, complete, knowing. We are Love.

Simply meditate on this symbol. Allow it to sink into your being. I am, I AM. This is who you are. This is your connection to all levels of your being and to the universe. Relax and follow where it takes you. I am, I AM. Know you will go exactly where you need to go, that all is in perfect order for you at this time. Trust. You have come far. You are always supported and loved. I am, I AM.

"The universe is saying: allow me to flow
through you unrestricted, and you will see
the greatest magic you have ever seen."
—Klaus Joehle

"Never apologize for shining your brightest,
the moon does it all the time and we
celebrate her."
—Spirit Daughter

"Everyone has their own path. Walk yours
with integrity and wish all others peace on
their journey. When your paths merge, rejoice
for their presence in your life. When the
paths are separated, return to the wholeness
of yourself, give thanks for the footprints
left on your soul, and embrace the time to
journey on your own."
—Phoebe Garnsworthy @lost_nowhere

"Life is too short to wake up in the morning
with regrets. So, love the people who treat
you right, forgive the ones who don't and
believe that everything happens for a reason.
If you get the chance, take it. If it changes
your life, let it. Nobody said it would be easy,
they just promised it would be worth it."
—Dr. Seuss

"We are shaped by our thoughts; we become
what we think. When the mind is pure, joy
follows like a shadow that never leaves."
—The Buddha

AFTERWORD

By Dr. Fiona Shamess
It has been a joy to read *The Little Book of Light Codes*. What an inspiration this book is! These symbols take us beyond our limited physical body and consciousness, into the limitless soul space. Chiropractic is all about mind-body connect, and these symbols take that one step farther...to mind/body/soul connect. This book is going to dovetail brilliantly with the work I do...I can hardly wait.

The Little Book of Light Codes is an extraordinary gift to the world. I am excited that something of such great value to all people is finally here. Laara, you have created perfect access to energetic healing. Bless you for making this book available to all sentient beings. It is the miracle we've been waiting for. Much gratitude,
—Dr. Fiona Shamess, Chiropractor, Victoria BC

POSTSCRIPT

I wish to thank you all for your bravery and openness in working through *The Little Book of Light Codes*. It is a true honor and privilege for me to share these symbols and accompanying messages with you. I hope you have found more joy and happiness by working with this book and that you will take your immeasurable Love out into the world to share with everyone. I wish you all the best on your continuing journey.

Until we meet again, blessings of Love and Light,
—Laara

REFERENCE

Green, Glenda. *Love Without End - Jesus Speaks*. Sedona: Spiritus, 1999.

(The "Love that we are" is a phrase used throughout *The Little Book of Light Codes* to help us remember that we are Love. I came across this phrase in the book "Love Without End" by Glenda Green. I encourage readers to read this very special book.)

ABOUT THE AUTHOR

Laara is a healing practitioner, channeler, and intuitive. Before focusing on energy and healing, for twenty years she competed up to an international level in the equestrian sport of show jumping. Now, she practices a variety of healing modalities, and continues to learn from acclaimed healer and teacher, Rosalyn L. Bruyere, and other cherished mentors. Laara enjoys practicing yoga, riding her horses, and living an ever-evolving, healthy and balanced lifestyle. Laara lives in Victoria, B.C. Canada. You can connect with her at: LightCodesByLaara.com

Made in the USA
Las Vegas, NV
05 December 2020